THE
UNOFFICIAL

KT-379-723

POKÉMON
GO
EXPERT
BATTLE
GUIDE

By Russ Murray

WELDONOWEN
PUBLISHING

First published in Great Britain in 2016 by Weldon Owen, an imprint of the Bonnier Publishing Group.

King's Road Publishing
3.08 The Plaza, 535 King's Road
Chelsea, London, SW10 0SZ

© 2016 Weldon Owen Ltd.
All rights reserved.

www.weldonowen.co.uk
www.bonnierpublishing.co.uk

Packaged by Cloud King Creative
www.cloudkingcreative.co.uk

ISBN: 978-1-7834-2461-0

First Edition
10 9 8 7 6 5 4 3 2 1
Printed in the UK

Weldon Owen Ltd
Publisher Donna Gregory
Editorial Fay Evans, Hazel Eriksson, Claire Phillip
Design Emma Vince, Shahid Mahmood

The information in this book has been carefully researched, and every reasonable effort has been made to ensure its accuracy. Neither the book's publisher nor its creators assume any responsibility for any accidents, injuries, losses or other damages that might come from its use. You are solely responsible for taking any and all reasonable and necessary precautions when performing the activities detailed in its pages.

Russfierce
& Pikachu

Me, Russ Murray!

Level 25

43358 / 190000 XP

THERE ARE MILLIONS of players who have been struggling to try and catch them all in Pokémon Go, and there is no doubt that this is still one of the most popular mobile apps available in the world. While the focus of the game is still about catching wild Pokémon, there is so much more to enjoy, which is why we have decided to share our expert tips on how to battle, win, and defend Gyms in Pokémon Go. With the knowledge contained in these pages, you can start to grow as a Pokémon Trainer, and continue your journey towards becoming a true Pokémon master. Knowledge really is the most vital part of your training, and with great wisdom will come bigger and better Pokémon, and of course rewards in the shape of extra experience, Stardust and PokéCoins for keeping hold of those Gyms. Get out there, get battling, and remember to have fun!

Russ

Russ Murray
Pokémon Master Trainer

TABLE OF CONTENTS

POWER UP YOUR PHONE

THE BEST WAYS TO PROLONG YOUR BATTERY LIFE AND STOP YOUR GAME FROM FREEZING AT THE CRUCIAL MOMENT!

HOW TO SAVE YOUR PHONE'S BATTERY

Because you need to have the app open in order to locate nearby Pokémon and log kilometres for hatching Eggs, Pokémon Go will drain your battery fairly quickly. While having a back-up power source and a charger on you is your best bet, here are some other tips to conserve battery power.

GENERAL PHONE TIPS

• Turn the brightness as low as it can go (without not being able to see the screen!).
• If you're using 3G or 4G, turn off wi-fi so your phone isn't searching for a signal.
• Find large public areas with free wi-fi to play, such as a shopping centre or park.
• If you're around any tall buildings or skyscrapers, they can cause your GPS signal to "bounce", tricking the phone into thinking that you're constantly on the move. This may help you when catching eggs.

SAVING YOUR DATA

Keep Pokémon Go from consuming a month's worth of data in one afternoon:

• Open Google Maps on your phone.
• Tap the Menu button.
• Navigate to the Settings menu.

• Tap on "Offline areas".
• Tap on the recommended "Home" region or use the "+" button in the bottom right-hand corner to select a specific area of the map, and then download.

FOR IPHONE

• Update to the latest version of iOS.
• Go to Settings > General > Background App Refresh and make sure it is turned off.
• Go to Settings > General > Siri and make sure it is turned off.
• Go to Settings > Privacy > Camera > Pokémon Go and make sure it is turned off.
• Go to Settings > Display & Brightness to turn off Auto-Brightness.
• Clear your RAM: Close all applications. On the home screen, hold down the Power button until the shutdown screen appears. Then hold down the Home button until the shutdown screen disappears.
• Completely close Pokémon Go by double clicking the Home button and swiping the app up. Turn on Airplane Mode, then open the app again. When you see a red bar that says "No Wi-Fi", swipe up from the bottom of your screen to open the Control Centre and turn off Airplane mode/turn on Wi-Fi.

POKÉSAFETY

STAY SAFE WHILE HUNTING AND BATTLING

MEETING OTHER PEOPLE

Though Pokémon Go is a fun way to meet other people, it's always a good idea to keep a few things in mind to stay safe.

1. Someone should always know where you are! If you aren't an adult yet, then always tell someone where you're going before you embark on a trip to the nearest Gym.

2. Never go anywhere with a stranger. You wouln't do it in real life, so don't do it for a Pokémon!

3. Stay together. If you go out Pokémon

hunting or searching for Gyms to Battle, go in a group. it's safer, and you'll have more fun.

4. As Pokémon Go reminds you, always pay attention to the world around you. Don't get so distracted by perfecting your dodge that you collide with other people or Trainers! Look up from your screen often.

6. If you're out trying to win and keep a Gym all day, make sure to dress appropriately for the weather, and take water and sunscreen.

7. If you're lucky enough to be able to drive around to find Pokémon Gyms, make sure to pull over safely before you start looking for Pokémon or starting a Battle.

8. Be careful when searching for Water-type Pokémon, or battling near bridges and crossings. You don't want to get too over-enthusiastic and throw your phone over the side!

9. If you're hunting or battling Pokémon out in the wild, in the park or the forest, then stick to the path! It's easy to get lost when you're not paying attention, and you don't want to disturb any real life animals.

10. Always check with the owner before you go onto someone else's property to try and catch Pokémon.

THE ROAD TO BECOMING A MASTER TRAINER

YOUR TRAINING STARTS HERE!

Whether you have been playing Pokémon Go for some time now or you are just a beginner, there are many ways to improve your skills, and this guide has been written to help you get the most out of the game. Whilst the focus of this handbook is primarily Gym Battles, we have also packed in plenty of other handy tips and tricks to help you hone your Trainer talents. So grab your phone and get ready to become a true Pokémon master!

THE BASICS

The main objective of the game is to catch and train Pokémon. Whether you have just thrown your first PokéBall or have assembled a good collection of Pokémon, there are always ways you can improve your catching technique. Every time you capture a Pokémon you will gain experience, Stardust, and Candies – and all of these are needed to improve and evolve your Pokémon, and increase your Trainer level.

THE CATCH

Catching Pokémon in the wild is a must in order to assemble a good team of Pokémon and earn experience. Every time you throw a PokéBall you have an opportunity to earn a little extra experience, and possibly improve your capture rate by adding a little curve to your throw. Curveballs may only add an additional 10 XP, but the capture rate is much better and so less Pokémon will flee from battles. By practicing your aim you can gain additional XP for getting the perfect throw. Land the PokéBall right in the centre of the capture circle and you can gain up to 100 extra XP for an exceptional throw. This may not seem like a lot, but it all mounts up and with a little practice you'll soon be earning plenty of XP.

Head outside and explore your local area to find and catch all sorts of amazing Pokémon.

POKÉMON		EGGS
142 / 250		9 / 9
CP 1517	CP 1312	CP 1312
Snorlax	Electabuzz	Golduck
CP 1298	CP 1159	CP 1024
Scyther	Hypno	Seaking
CP 994	CP 940	CP 900
Kingler	Jynx	Starmie
CP 887	CP 879	CP 877
Lapras		

A mix of different Pokémon will ensure you have a winnng team.

EVOLVING

Once you have caught a small ensemble of Pokémon, you will want to start evolving them to make them stronger and more powerful. In order to evolve your Pokémon you need to collect Candies, and these can be gained by capturing Pokémon, but also by transferring your weaker Pokémon to Professor Willow. Take a look at the amount of Candies needed to evolve each Pokémon and save your highest CP Pokémon for evolution purposes. This way you will save a lot of Candies that you'll need to power them up later.

POWERING UP YOUR POKÉMON

In order to power up your Pokémon you need both Candies and Stardust. The stronger your Pokémon is, the more Stardust will be required to increase its stats. Make sure you only evolve your very strongest Pokémon, and this way you'll end up with a great team of Pokémon that require minimal powering up once evolved.

CP 1462

Gyarados

HP 119 / 119

Water / Flying	235kg	7.9 m
Type	Weight	Height

18977
STARDUST

16
MAGIKARP CANDY

POWER UP   2500   2

6

Power up your Pokémon using a combination of Stardust and Candy.

MASTER TRAINER GEAR

THE TOOLS OF THE TRADE!

As you start to improve your Trainer's level by capturing Pokémon, lots of cool new gear will become available to you. This new equipment will help to make catching Pokémon even easier, and will enable you to grow towards your goal of becoming a formidable Pokémon master.

RAZZ BERRIES

Razz Berries become available once you reach Trainer level 8. This special fruit is collected at PokéStops and is used to make the encountered Pokémon like you a little more. Once feeding the Pokémon a Razz Berry, a small heart symbol will appear next to the Pokémon, and it is less likely to run away while you are trying to capture it.

GREAT BALLS

Great Balls become available to you once you reach Trainer level 12. These are also collected from PokéStops and have a more successful capture rate than the standard PokéBall. It is best to save these balls for Pokémon with higher CP or for Pokémon that you do not want to escape. When combined with a Razz Berry the Great Ball will greatly increase your capture success.

ULTRA BALLS

Ultra Balls do not become available until you reach Trainer level 20. These are even better than Great Balls for capturing those high CP Pokémon. Once again, when used in combination with a Razz Berry, Great Balls will provide you with a higher success rate when capturing rare and hard-to-find Pokémon. Save these balls for the most difficult to catch Pokémon.

Give a Pokémon a Razz Berry and it's less likely to evade capture.

Level up to access more items. **Try Great Balls over PokéBalls.** **Carry more with the Bag Upgrade.**

MASTER BALLS

Master Balls are the ultimate catching device, but are not available to you until you reach Trainer level 30. Again, they can be collected from PokéStops once you reach the required level and these will help you to catch those really rare and almost impossible-to-find Pokémon. Using a Master Ball does not guarantee success, but does significantly improve your chances.

UPGRADES

In the shop there are some other essential upgrades that will help you to become a master Trainer. In particular the Bag Upgrade and the Pokémon Storage Upgrade will be essential purchases once you have earned yourself plenty of PokéCoins. Increasing the number of items you can carry will benefit you greatly later in the game enabling you to carry more Balls, Razz Berries, Potions, and Revives.

The Pokémon Storage Upgrade is essential once your collection of captures begins to grow.

NEW UPDATES

THE GAME IS EVOLVING

MEDAL SYSTEM

In a recent update to Pokémon Go, players are now rewarded for collecting medals. Previously these medals only served as achievements for catching certain types of Pokémon, but now Catch Bonuses are being awarded for each Pokémon caught depending on the level of medal you have unlocked. According to research, these Catch Bonuses will increase your chance of catching more Pokémon of that type.

Medal	Activity	Bronze (Catch Bonus)	Silver (Catch Bonus)	Gold (Catch Bonus)
Schoolkid	Catch Normal-type Pokémon	10 (+1)	50 (+2)	200 (+3)
Black Belt	Catch Fighting-type Pokémon	10 (+1)	50 (+2)	200 (+3)
Bird Keeper	Catch Flying-type Pokémon	10 (+1)	50 (+2)	200 (+3)
Punk Girl	Catch Poison-type Pokémon	10 (+1)	50 (+2)	200 (+3)
Ruin Maniac	Catch Ground-type Pokémon	10 (+1)	50 (+2)	200 (+3)
Hiker	Catch Rock-type Pokémon	10 (+1)	50 (+2)	200 (+3)
Bug Catcher	Catch Bug-type Pokémon	10 (+1)	50 (+2)	200 (+3)
Hex Maniac	Catch Ghost-type Pokémon	10 (+1)	50 (+2)	200 (+3)
Depot Agent	Catch Steel-type Pokémon	10 (+1)	50 (+2)	200 (+3)
Kindler	Catch Fire-type Pokémon	10 (+1)	50 (+2)	200 (+3)
Swimmer	Catch Water-type Pokémon	10 (+1)	50 (+2)	200 (+3)
Gardener	Catch Grass-type Pokémon	10 (+1)	50 (+2)	200 (+3)
Rocker	Catch Electric-type Pokémon	10 (+1)	50 (+2)	200 (+3)
Psychic	Catch Psychic-type Pokémon	10 (+1)	50 (+2)	200 (+3)
Skier	Catch Ice-type Pokémon	10 (+1)	50 (+2)	200 (+3)
Dragon Tamer	Catch Dragon-type Pokémon	10 (+1)	50 (+2)	200 (+3)
Fairy Tale Girl	Catch Fairy-type Pokémon	10 (+1)	50 (+2)	200 (+3)

SPECIAL EVENTS

As of Halloween 2016, Pokémon Go will feature themed events for special occasions. This hugely successful first Halloween event featured more "spooky" Pokémon to catch, six candies rewarded for each Pokémon and other bonuses. There has been speculation that due to the success of first event, Niantic may follow up with a Christmas themed event, perhaps with an abundance of Ice-type Pokémon?

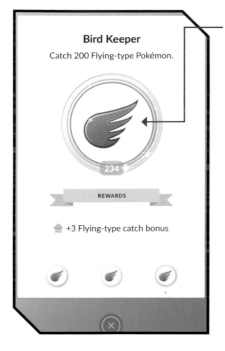

Bird Keeper

Catch 200 Flying-type Pokémon.

234

REWARDS

+3 Flying-type catch bonus

Collect lots of one kind of Pokémon to receive a special Catch Bonus.

HOW TO RECOGNIZE THE PROS

Your Team Leader will give you plenty of information on your Pokémon during the appraisal, but you are really just looking for one of a few key phrases that will signify that your Pokémon is one of the elite. Pay close attention and look out for any of the following phrases, and then focus your attention on the Pokémon that pass the test.

"Your Pokémon is a wonder!", "Your Pokémon simply amazes me", "Your Pokémon looks like it can really battle with the best of them!"

APPRAISING YOUR POKÉMON

In another recent update to the game, you can now have each of your Pokémon appraised by your Team Leader. At first look this may seem like a pointless exercise, but it is in fact the key to determining which Pokémon are going to be the best for evolving and using for battling. Not all Pokémon are created equally, and each and every Pokémon in the game has unique hidden individual values (IV). These hidden stats hold the clues to the Pokémon's potential, and by appraising your Pokémon you can easily work out which ones are worth spending time developing and evolving. Pokémon that do not measure up can instantly be transferred, as there is no way to improve these hidden stats. They either have the skills or they don't!

CP 297

Charmeleon

HP45/45

Fire
Type

20.06kg
Weight

37837
STARDUST

POWER

Overall, your Charmeleon looks like it can really battle with the best of them!

Team Leaders will tell you how tough your Pokémon are.

BUDDY SYSTEM

TAKE A POKÉBUDDY WITH YOU ON YOUR TRAVELS AND YOU'LL BE REWARDED WITH MORE CANDIES.

In a recent update to Pokémon Go, its developers have introduced a new Buddy System to the game. This fun new game mechanic enables players to choose a Pokémon from their captured list, and walk with it to earn extra Candies. In order to help you make the right choice when picking the perfect partner, we have devised this chart showing how far each Pokémon must be walked in order to collect a Candy.

SELECTING YOUR BUDDY
To choose your partner simply follow these simple steps:

1. Select your Trainer avatar in the lower left hand corner of the screen.

2. Select the menu button in the lower right-hand corner of the Trainer screen.

3. Select the Buddy option to choose your partner.

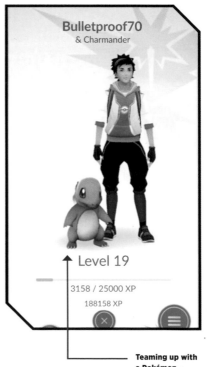

Bulletproof70
& Charmander

Level 19

3158 / 25000 XP

188158 XP

Teaming up with a Pokémon Buddy will earn you more Candy.

POKÉMON SIZE

The size of the Pokémon you choose as your Buddy will determine where it stands in relation to your Trainer on your profile screen. Some (such as Pikachu) will sit on your shoulder, whilst others are far too big so will stand beside or behind you.

LOW MILEAGE POKÉMON

These Pokémon require only one kilometre of walking to grab a Candy.

No.	Name	KM for 1 Candy	Size
10	CATERPIE	1	Shoulder
11	METAPOD	1	Medium
12	BUTTERFREE	1	Flying
13	WEEDLE	1	Shoulder
14	KAKUNA	1	Medium
15	BEEDRILL	1	Flying
16	PIDGEY	1	Shoulder
17	PIDGEOTTO	1	Flying
18	PIDGEOT	1	Flying
19	RATTATA	1	Medium
20	RATICATE	1	Medium
21	SPEAROW	1	Shoulder
22	FEAROW	1	Flying
25	PIKACHU	1	Shoulder
26	RAICHU	1	Medium
35	CLEFAIRY	1	Medium
36	CLEFABLE	1	Big
39	JIGGLYPUFF	1	Medium
40	WIGGLYTUFF	1	Big
41	ZUBAT	1	Flying
42	GOLBAT	1	Flying
74	GEODUDE	1	Medium
75	GRAVELER	1	Big
76	GOLEM	1	Big
129	MAGIKARP	1	Medium
130	GYARADOS	1	Big

Walk the required number of km to gain valuable Candy.

MEDIUM MILEAGE POKÉMON

These Pokémon must be walked for three kilometres to receive a Candy.

No.	Name	KM for 1 Candy	Size	No.	Name	KM for 1 Candy	Size
1	BULBASAUR	3	Medium	71	VICTREEBEL	3	Big
2	IVYSAUR	3	Big	72	TENTACOOL	3	Medium
3	VENUSAUR	3	Big	73	TENTACRUEL	3	Big
4	CHARMANDER	3	Medium	77	PONYTA	3	Medium
5	CHARMELEON	3	Medium	78	RAPIDASH	3	Big
6	CHARIZARD	3	Big	79	SLOWPOKE	3	Medium
7	SQUIRTLE	3	Medium	80	SLOWBRO	3	Big
8	WARTORTLE	3	Medium	81	MAGNEMITE	3	Flying
9	BLASTOISE	3	Big	82	MAGNETON	3	Big
23	EKANS	3	Medium	83	FARFETCH'D	3	Medium
24	ARBOK	3	Big	84	DODUO	3	Medium
27	SANDSHREW	3	Medium	85	DODRIO	3	Big
28	SANDSLASH	3	Medium	86	SEEL	3	Medium
29	NIDORAN F	3	Medium	87	DEWGONG	3	Medium
30	NIDORINA	3	Medium	88	GRIMER	3	Medium
31	NIDOQUEEN	3	Big	89	MUK	3	Big
32	NIDORAN M	3	Medium	90	SHELLDER	3	Medium
33	NIDORINO	3	Medium	91	CLOYSTER	3	Big
34	NIDOKING	3	Big	92	GASTLY	3	Flying
37	VULPIX	3	Medium	93	HAUNTER	3	Flying
38	NINETALES	3	Big	94	GENGAR	3	Big
43	ODDISH	3	Medium	95	ONIX	5	Big
44	GLOOM	3	Medium	96	DROWZEE	3	Big
45	VILEPLUME	3	Big	97	HYPNO	3	Big
46	PARAS	3	Medium	98	KRABBY	3	Medium
47	PARASECT	3	Medium	99	KINGLER	3	Big
48	VENONAT	3	Medium	100	VOLTORB	3	Medium
49	VENOMOTH	3	Flying	101	ELECTRODE	3	Big
50	DIGLETT	3	Medium	102	EXEGGCUTE	3	Medium
51	DUGTRIO	3	Big	103	EXEGGUTOR	3	Big
52	MEOWTH	3	Medium	104	CUBONE	3	Medium
53	PERSIAN	3	Medium	105	MAROWAK	3	Medium
54	PSYDUCK	3	Medium	108	LICKITUNG	3	Medium
55	GOLDUCK	3	Big	109	KOFFING	3	Big
56	MANKEY	3	Medium	110	WEEZING	3	Big
57	PRIMEAPE	3	Big	111	RHYHORN	3	Big
58	GROWLITHE	3	Medium	112	RHYDON	3	Big
59	ARCANINE	3	Big	114	TANGELA	3	Medium
60	POLIWAG	3	Medium	115	KANGASKHAN	3	Big
61	POLIWHIRL	3	Big	116	HORSEA	3	Medium
62	POLIWRATH	3	Big	117	SEADRA	3	Big
63	ABRA	3	Medium	118	GOLDEEN	3	Medium
64	KADABRA	3	Big	119	SEAKING	3	Big
65	ALAKAZAM	3	Big	120	STARYU	3	Medium
66	MACHOP	3	Medium	121	STARMIE	3	Big
67	MACHOKE	3	Big	128	TAUROS	3	Big
68	MACHAMP	3	Big	132	DITTO	3	Medium
69	BELLSPROUT	3	Medium	137	PORYGON	3	Big
70	WEEPINBELL	3	Big				

HIGH MILEAGE POKÉMON

Walk five kilometres with these Pokémon to grab a Candy.

No.	Name	KM for 1 Candy	Size
106	HITMONLEE	5	Big
107	HITMONCHAN	5	Big
113	CHANSEY	5	Big
122	MR. MIME	5	Medium
123	SCYTHER	5	Big
124	JYNX	5	Big
125	ELECTABUZZ	5	Medium
126	MAGMAR	5	Big
127	PINSIR	5	Big
131	LAPRAS	5	Big
133	EEVEE	5	Shoulder
134	VAPOREON	5	Medium
135	JOLTEON	5	Medium
136	FLAREON	5	Medium
138	OMANYTE	5	Medium
139	OMASTAR	5	Big
140	KABUTO	5	Medium
141	KABUTOPS	5	Big
142	AERODACTYL	5	Big
143	SNORLAX	5	Big
144	ARTICUNO	5	Flying
145	ZAPDOS	5	Flying
146	MOLTRES	5	Big
147	DRATINI	5	Medium
148	DRAGONAIR	5	Big
149	DRAGONITE	5	Big
150	MEWTWO	5	Big
151	MEW	5	Medium

CP 554

Hitmonlee ✏

HP 56 / 56

Fighting	57.54 kg	1.4 m
Type	Weight	Height

10347
STARDUST

18
HITMONLEE CANDY

POWER UP   1900   2

✕   ??Attack??   5

Choose Hitmonlee and receive a Candy every 5 km!

MAXIMIZING STARDUST

HOW TO MAKE THE MOST OF YOUR STARDUST

Stardust is one of the most important things to collect in Pokémon Go, as it is necessary in order to power up your Pokémon. However, it is not that easy to get and it can take quite a long time to build up enough Stardust to be able to give power to the Pokémon that need it.

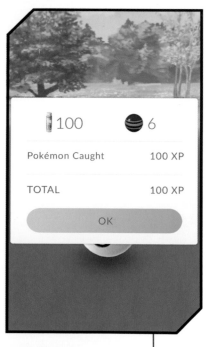

Receive Stardust every time you catch a Pokémon.

CATCHING

The easiest way to earn Stardust is to catch wild Pokémon. For every successful capture you will gain 100 Stardust, and while this does not seem like a lot, it will soon mount up if you save it. Of course Pokémon Go is all about capturing wild Pokémon, so you'll be earning a lot of Stardust in this way. There are a few ways you can increase the amount of captures you make, and therefore increase the Stardust you receive too.

Glowing pink PokéStops are a sign of an active Lure.

Additional Lures can be bought from the shop.

LURES

Using Lures on PokéStops is a great way to attract more Pokémon to the area you are currently in. Each Lure lasts for exactly 30 minutes, and will continue to attract wild Pokémon towards the PokéStop. Once the Lure is active, the PokéStop will start glowing and emit a pink sparkly mist attracting a new Pokémon to the PokéStop once every five minutes. As an added bonus, you can also keep collecting items from the PokéStop every five minutes.

Lures are a great way to meet friends and capture Pokémon together. In towns and cities there are many places where there are groups of PokéStops close together, and these make great places to drop Lures. Sitting in the centre of a group of Lures can be really beneficial to your catching lots of Pokémon and also meeting new friends. Look out for PokéStops with Lures already active on them, and sit by them for great results.

Boost your chances of finding Pokémon by using Incense.

INCENSE

Incense is another great way to increase the amount of Pokémon you can catch, by attracting wild Pokémon to your position as you walk around. The key to getting the most from Incense is to walk around, as the amount of Pokémon you'll encounter will increase dramatically the more you move. Sitting still with Incense will cause an additional Pokémon to spawn once every five minutes. However, if walking with Incense, a new Pokémon will appear every 200 metres walked. For the best results, combine an Incense with a Lucky Egg and go for a long stroll. You will not only catch plenty of Pokémon, but also gain double XP and get more mileage on your Eggs and for your Buddy.

EGGS

One of the very best ways to earn extra Stardust is to hatch Pokémon from Eggs. Hatching a 10 km Egg can net you up to 2000 Stardust in one go, with rewards slightly less for the 5 km and 2 km Eggs. However, by buying more Incubators you can be walking and hatching up to nine Eggs at a time. This will generate plenty of Stardust and also the chance of hatching some rarer Pokémon at the same time.

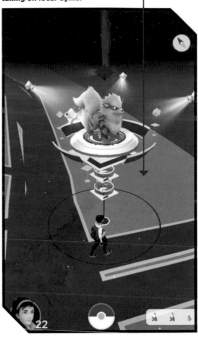

Earn additional Stardust by taking on local Gyms.

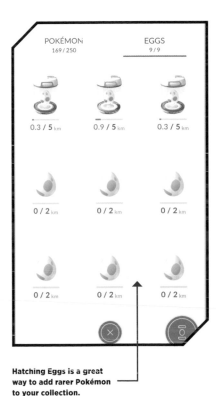

Hatching Eggs is a great way to add rarer Pokémon to your collection.

GYMS

The final way to earn more Stardust in Pokémon Go is by taking on Gyms. Of course we will be covering this in a lot more detail later on in this guide, but for now all you need to know is that for successfully holding on to a Gym you will be rewarded with PokéCoins and 500 Stardust for each Gym held.

POKÉMON GO PLUS

POWER UP YOUR POKÉMON GO

Pokémon Go Plus is a smart device that enables you to play Pokémon Go without having to constantly have your phone in your hand. The device clips to a bag strap or your wrist and can be used to collect items from PokéStops, catch wild Pokémon, and even hatch eggs.

PAIRING YOUR DEVICE

In order for Pokémon Go Plus to work with your app, you must first pair the device with your phone via its Bluetooth connection. Before you start, make sure you are running the latest version of Pokémon Go and then click on the settings menu. Select Pokémon Go Plus and this will pair your device with your phone. Once this is done you'll be ready to start using the Pokémon Go Plus.

CAPTURING POKÉMON WITH POKÉMON GO PLUS

Pokémon Go Plus enables you to capture Pokémon without the need to remove your phone from your pocket. When a Pokémon is detected, the Pokémon Go Plus will vibrate once and a green light will flash to notify you that there is a Pokémon nearby. Simply press the button on the Pokémon Go Plus and it will attempt a capture. If successful, the Pokémon Go Plus will flash white and vibrate three times followed by multi-coloured lights and vibrations. If unsuccessful the Pokémon Go Plus will still flash white with vibrations, but will then display a red LED to signify that the Pokémon was not caught.

NOTE: Pokémon Go Plus will only use standard PokéBalls to attempt to capture Pokémon. If you want to use Razz Berries or other balls, you will need to use your phone directly.

COLLECTING ITEMS WITH POKÉMON GO PLUS

When using Pokémon Go Plus, every time you pass a PokéStop the device will vibrate twice and flash a blue LED. Simply press the button at this time and the Pokémon Go Plus will collect all the items available for you at the PokéStop. The Pokémon Go Plus will vibrate once for each item collected in this way. If your Bag is full and there is no room to collect more items, the Pokémon Go Plus will vibrate once and display a white LED.

HATCHING EGGS WITH POKÉMON GO PLUS

While it was initially believed that Pokémon Go Plus would not track distance covered for hatching Eggs and earning Candy with your Buddy, this is not the case. The Pokémon Go Plus still tracks the distance walked, even while your phone is asleep in your pocket. However, you will not receive a notification of any Eggs hatched or Candies earned until you next look at the app itself.

EXPERT ADVICE

You can now select one of multiple notification modes. The default setting notifies you of wild Pokémon and PokéStops, but these can now be turned off individually. The update also prevents the need to re-pair your device and Pokémon Go Plus every time you use the app.

CHOOSING A TEAM

WHO WILL YOU CHOOSE?

Once you reach level 5, and before taking on your first Gym, you will face an important decision – which team to represent. There are three teams to choose from in the game, and whilst each has a slightly different philosophy, the choice is really a rather personal one. However, choose wisely as you will not be able to change teams once you have made your selection. Here is some information about the three teams to help you make that all-important decision.

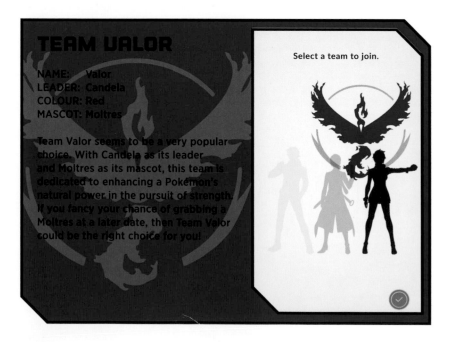

TEAM VALOR

NAME: Valor
LEADER: Candela
COLOUR: Red
MASCOT: Moltres

Team Valor seems to be a very popular choice. With Candela as its leader and Moltres as its mascot, this team is dedicated to enhancing a Pokémon's natural power in the pursuit of strength. If you fancy your chance of grabbing a Moltres at a later date, then Team Valor could be the right choice for you!

Select a team to join.

TEAM INSTINCT

NAME: Instinct
LEADER: Blanche
COLOUR: Yellow
MASCOT: Articuno

Team Instinct seems to be an equally popular choice. Led by Blanche and with Articuno as its mascot, this team is dedicated to the wisdom of Pokémon and hopes that analysis of every situation will help win the day. If you're hoping to grab an Articuno at some point, then Team Instinct might be the one for you to align with!

Select a team to join.

TEAM MYSTIC

NAME: Mystic
LEADER: Spark
COLOUR: Blue
MASCOT: Zapdos

Team Mystic appears to be the least popular of the three teams, but that does not mean they are a bad choice. Led by Spark and with Zapdos as its mascot, this team is dedicated to the intuition of Pokémon. If you'd like to eventually add a Zapdos to your collection, Team Mystic could be the right one for you to select!

Select a team to join.

POKÉMON LINE-UP

ASSEMBLING A TEAM TO TAKE ON THE GYMS

Assembling a good team of Pokémon is really important, as this will help you to tackle Gyms, and start earning PokéCoins. While you will be restricted to the Pokémon commonly found in your local area, there are several ways you can increase the number of Pokémon you have in your team. To be successful you really need to try and get a strong mix of different Pokémon types, as this is the key to making the Gym battles easier.

HATCHING EGGS

One of the best ways to get your hands on rare Pokémon is to hatch them from the Eggs you can collect at PokéStops. Whilst you have one Incubator that is always available, you can buy extra Incubators from the Shop and hatch multiple Eggs at the same time.

Egg Incubator

A device that incubates an Egg as you walk until it is ready to hatch. Breaks after 3 uses.

EXCHANGE FOR   150

You'll eventually need more than one Incubator to keep hatching Eggs.

EXPERT ADVICE

Discovering everything that Pokémon Go has to offer requires a lot of walking and travelling. Make sure you get out and about frequently and visit plenty of different areas to catch different types of Pokémon.

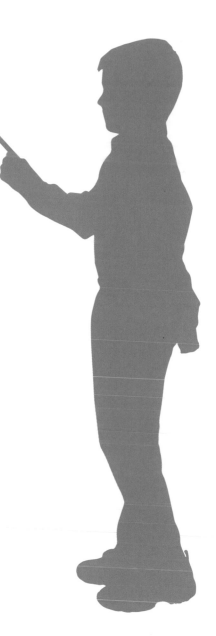

A GOOD MIX

In order to be successful at taking on Gyms and winning battles, you will need a varied team of Pokémon. Just like in the Game Boy and Nintendo DS games, Pokémon Go plays on the strengths and weaknesses of different Pokémon types, and in order to win you will need to understand which Pokémon will work best against opposing types. Remember, a Pokémon that is strong where another is weak will do double damage, making winning that much easier. To help you we have compiled a list of the top ten Pokémon for attack, defence, HP, and overall.

Blastoise is one of the best
Water-type Pokémon to
evolve, capture, or hatch.

CP 322

Blastoise ✏

HP 48 / 48

Water	86.77 kg	1.52 m
Type	Weight	Height

1230
STARDUST

3
BLASTOISE CANDY

POWER UP   600   1

10

For a true Pokémon
powerhouse, a Dragonite
is tough to beat.

CP 1127

Dragonite ✏

HP 84 / 84

Dragon / Flying	383.32 kg	2.8 m
Type	Weight	Height

8717
STARDUST

0
DRATINI CANDY

POWER UP   1300   2

TOP 10 ATTACK POKÉMON

Here are the best Pokémon,
based on their attack stats.

1	DRAGONITE	250
2	FLAREON	238
3	EXEGGUTOR	232
4	ARCANINE	230
5	VICTREEBEL	222
6	CHARIZARD	212
7	MAGMAR	214
8	GENGAR	204
9	NIDOKING	204
10	VILEPLUME	202

TOP 10 DEFENCE POKÉMON

Here are the top 10 Pokémon
based on their defence stats.

1	BLASTOISE	222
2	DRAGONITE	212
3	HITMONCHAN	204
4	POLIWRATH	202
5	OMASTAR	202
6	MAROWAK	202
7	VENUSAUR	200
8	SLOWBRO	198
9	WEEZING	198
10	GOLEM	198

This sleepy Pokémon is second only to a Dragonite in overall stats.

CP 1104

Snorlax ✏

HP 156 / 156

Normal	422.21 kg	2.08 m
Type	Weight	Height

🔋110
STARDUST

🍬 10
SNORLAX CANDY

POWER UP   🔋1300   🍬 2

10

Chanseys can be suprisingly effective in battles due to their high HP stats.

CP 28

Chansey ✏

HP 84 / 84

Normal	35.65 kg	1.09 m
Type	Weight	Height

🔋471
STARDUST

🍬 32
CHANSEY CANDY

POWER UP   🔋200   🍬 1

15

TOP 10 HIT POINTS POKÉMON

Here are the top 10 Pokémon based on their HP stats.

1	CHANSEY	500
2	SNORLAX	320
3	WIGGLYTUFF	280
4	LAPRAS	260
5	VAPOREON	260
6	JIGGLYPUFF	230
7	RHYDON	160
8	KANGASKHAN	210
9	MUK	210
10	SLOWBRO	190

TOP 10 OVERALL POKÉMON

Here are the top 10 Pokémon based on their overall stats.

1	DRAGONITE
2	SNORLAX
3	LAPRAS
4	ARCANINE
5	BLASTOISE
6	EXEGGUTOR
7	VAPOREON
8	GYARADOS
9	SLOWBRO
10	VENUSAUR

SETTING UP YOUR TEAM

THE DREAM TEAM

The most important thing in Pokémon Go is your Pokémon. You need to study them, train them, evolve them, and power them up to get them to be the best they can be, and there is always so much you can learn. Careful inspection of the Pokémon you have at your disposal can help you assemble a team to take on any challenge.

STUDY YOUR POKÉMON CAREFULLY

Take a really good look at your Pokémon and make sure you only evolve the very best ones, so reserve your Candy for powering them up. Use the appraisal system to highlight the top-tier Pokémon, and then mark them as favourites so you can clearly identify them. Don't waste Candies on powering up a Pokémon at its early stage of evolution. Always wait until it reaches its highest evolution, as you will then know whether it has gained the best moves or not. It's a good idea to know what the best moves are for each Pokémon too, so this chart should help.

Pokémon	Best Quick Move	Best Main Move
BULBASAUR	Vine Whip	Power Whip
IVYSAUR	Vine Whip	Solar Beam
VENUSAUR	Vine Whip	Solar Beam
CHARMANDER	Scratch	Flamethrower
CHARMELEON	Scratch	Flamethrower
CHARIZARD	Wing Attack	Fire Blast
SQUIRTLE	Bubble	Aqua Tail
WARTORTLE	Water Gun	Hydro Pump
BLASTOISE	Water Gun	Hydro Pump
CATERPIE	Bug Bite	Struggle
METAPOD	Bug Bite	Struggle
BUTTERFREE	Bug Bite	Bug Buzz
WEEDLE	Bug Bite	Struggle
KAKUNA	Bug Bite	Struggle
BEEDRILL	Poison Jab	Sludge Bomb
PIDGEY	Tackle	Aerial Ace
PIDGEOTTO	Wing Attack	Aerial Ace
PIDGEOT	Wing Attack	Hurricane
RATTATA	Tackle	Body Slam
RATICATE	Bite	Hyper Beam
SPEAROW	Peck	Drill Peck
FEAROW	Steel Wing	Drill Run
EKANS	Poison Sting	Gunk Shot
ARBOK	Bite	Gunk Shot
PIKACHU	Thunder Shock	Thunder
RAICHU	Spark	Thunder
SANDSHREW	Mud Shot	Dig
SANDSLASH	Mud Shot	Earthquake
NIDORAN (F)	Poison Sting	Sludge Bomb
NIDORINA	Poison Sting	Sludge Bomb
NIDOQUEEN	Poison Jab	Earthquake
NIDORAN (M)	Poison Sting	Body Slam
NIDORINO	Poison Jab	Sludge Bomb
NIDOKING	Poison Jab	Earthquake
CLEFAIRY	Pound	Moonblast
CLEFABLE	Pound	Moonblast
VULPIX	Ember	Flamethrower

Pokémon	Best Quick Move	Best Main Move
NINETALES	Ember	Fire Blast
JIGGLYPUFF	Pound	Body Slam
WIGGLYTUFF	Pound	Hyper Beam
ZUBAT	Bite	Sludge Bomb
GOLBAT	Wing Attack	Air Cutter
ODDISH	Razor Leaf	Sludge Bomb
GLOOM	Razor Leaf	Sludge Bomb
VILEPLUME	Razor Leaf	Solar Beam
PARAS	Bug Bite	Seed Bomb
PARASECT	Bug Bite	Solar Beam
VENONAT	Bug Bite	Signal Beam
VENOMOTH	Bug Bite	Bug Buzz
DIGLETT	Mud Slap	Dig
DUGTRIO	Mud Slap	Stone Edge
MEOWTH	Scratch	Body Slam
PERSIAN	Scratch	Play Rough
PSYDUCK	Water Gun	Cross Chop
GOLDUCK	Water Gun	Hydro Pump
MANKEY	Scratch	Cross Chop
PRIMEAPE	Low Kick	Cross Chop
GROWLITHE	Bite	Flamethrower
ARCANINE	Fire Fang	Fire Blast
POLIWAG	Bubble	Body Slam
POLIWHIRL	Bubble	Scald
POLIWRATH	Bubble	Hydro Pump
ABRA	Zen Headbutt	Psyshock
KADABRA	Psycho Cut	Shadow Ball
ALAKAZAM	Psycho Cut	Psychic
MACHOP	Low Kick	Cross Chop
MACHOKE	Low Kick	Cross Chop
MACHAMP	Karate Chop	Cross Chop
BELLSPROUT	Vine Whip	Power Whip
WEEPINBELL	Razor Leaf	Power Whip
VICTREEBEL	Razor Leaf	Solar Beam
TENTACOOL	Bubble	Water Pulse
TENTACRUEL	Poison Jab	Hydro Pump
GEODUDE	Rock Throw	Rock Slide
GRAVELER	Mud Slap	Stone Edge
GOLEM	Mud Slap	Stone Edge
PONYTA	Ember	Fire Blast
RAPIDASH	Ember	Fire Blast
SLOWPOKE	Water Gun	Psychic
SLOWBRO	Water Gun	Psychic
MAGNEMITE	Spark	Thunderbolt
MAGNETON	Spark	Flash Cannon
FARFETCH'D	Cut	Leaf Blade
DODUO	Peck	Drill Peck
DODRIO	Feint Attack	Drill Peck
SEEL	Ice Shard	Aqua Tail
DEWGONG	Frost Breath	Blizzard
GRIMER	Poison Jab	Sludge Bomb
MUK	Poison Jab	Gunk Shot
SHELLDER	Tackle	Water Pulse
CLOYSTER	Frost Breath	Blizzard

CP 237

Aerodactyl

HP 56 / 56

Rock/Flying · 70.83kg · 1.87m
Type · Weight · Height

15819 STARDUST · 3 AERODACTYL CANDY

POWER UP · 800 · 1

6

Aerodactyl's best main move is Hyper Beam.

CP 32

Venusaur

HP 16 / 16

Grass/Poison · 123.69kg · 2.1m
Type · Weight · Height

14402 STARDUST · 18 BULBASAUR CANDY

POWER UP · 200 · 1

10

Venusaur's Vine Whip is its best quick move.

CP 11

Pikachu ✎

HP 10 / 10

Electric | 10.1 kg | 0.5 m
Type | Weight | Height

⚡ 100
STARDUST

🍬 3
PIKACHU CANDY

POWER UP | ⚡ 200 | 🍬 1

EVOLVE | 🍬 50

Pikachu's Thunder Shock
is a great quick move.

CP 353

Wartortle ✎

HP 51 / 51

Water | 6.84 kg | 0.86
Type | Weight | Height

⚡ 43813
STARDUST

🍬 2
SQUIRTLE CANDY

POWER UP | ⚡ 1000 | 🍬 1

EVOLVE | 🍬 100

Try Wartortle's Hydro
Pump main move.

Pokémon	Best Quick Move	Best Main Move
GASTLY	Lick	Sludge Bomb
HAUNTER	Shadow Claw	Sludge Bomb
GENGAR	Shadow Claw	Sludge Bomb
ONIX	Rock Throw	Stone Edge
DROWZEE	Pound	Psychic
HYPNO	Zen Headbutt	Psychic
KRABBY	Bubble	Water Pulse
KINGLER	Metal Claw	X Scissor
VOLTORB	Spark	Thunderbolt
ELECTRODE	Spark	Hyper Beam
EXEGGCUTE	Confusion	Psychic
EXEGGUTOR	Zen Headbutt	Solar Beam
CUBONE	Mud Slap	Bone Club
MAROWAK	Mud Slap	Earthquake
HITMONLEE	Rock Smash	Stone Edge
HITMONCHAN	Rock Smash	Brick Break
LICKITUNG	Zen Headbutt	Hyper Beam
KOFFING	Tackle	Sludge Bomb
WEEZING	Tackle	Sludge Bomb
RHYHORN	Mud Slap	Stomp
RHYDON	Mud Slap	Stone Edge
CHANSEY	Pound	Hyper Beam
TANGELA	Vine Whip	Solar Beam
KANGASKHAN	Mud Slap	Earthquake
HORSEA	Water Gun	Dragon Pulse
SEADRA	Water Gun	Hydro Pump
GOLDEEN	Mud Shot	Aqua Tail
SEAKING	Poison Jab	Megahorn
STARYU	Water Gun	Power Gem
STARMIE	Water Gun	Hydro Pump
MR. MIME	Zen Headbutt	Psychic
SCYTHER	Steel Wing	Bug Buzz
JYNX	Frost Breath	Psyshock
ELECTABUZZ	Thunder Shock	Thunder
MAGMAR	Ember	Fire Blast
PINSIR	Rock Smash	X Scissor
TAUROS	Tackle	Earthquake
MAGIKARP	Splash	Struggle
GYARADOS	Bite	Hydro Pump
LAPRAS	Frost Breath	Blizzard
EEVEE	Tackle	Body Slam
VAPOREON	Water Gun	Hydro Pump
JOLTEON	Thunder Shock	Thunder
FLAREON	Ember	Fire Blast
PORYGON	Tackle	Signal Beam
OMANYTE	Water Gun	Ancient Power
OMASTAR	Water Gun	Hydro Pump
KABUTO	Scratch	Aqua Jet
KABUTOPS	Mud Shot	Stone Edge
AERODACTYL	Bite	Hyper Beam
SNORLAX	Zen Headbutt	Body Slam
DRATINI	Dragon Breath	Aqua Tail
DRAGONAIR	Dragon Breath	Dragon Pulse
DRAGONITE	Dragon Breath	Dragon Claw

Take a look at what
moves your evolved
Pokémon has gained.

NAME YOUR TEAM

Once you have decided the Pokémon you want to use for each team, you'll want to make it easy to find them for quick selection when in Gyms or training. The easiest way to do this is to change the name of your Pokémon. You can add or change the name text to anything you like, and if you add a symbol like an exclamation mark at the start, these Pokémon will always appear at the top of your list too. We suggest a simple system like !A Hypno , !D Snorlax, !P Sandslash etc.

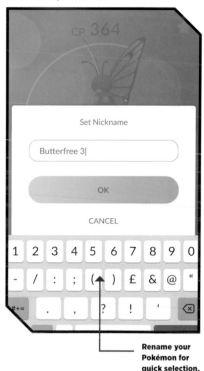

DECIDE THEIR FATE

Once you have evolved your Pokémon, you'll then see what moves they have gained, and whether they will be better suited to an attacking or a defensive role. They might also have low CP, which may make them particularly useful for power Prestige Gyms. Now is the time to decide what you want to do with them, and sort them into teams ATK (attack), DEF (defence), and PTG (Prestige Gym).

Rename your
Pokémon for
quick selection.

TEAM CARE

LOOK AFTER YOUR POKÉMON

After every battle, it's good practice to revive your fainted Pokémon and heal those injured in battle, so they are ready to fight again. There are a number of items available to help you do this, and these get better as you gain in Trainer rank.

POTIONS

The Potion is the most basic healing, as it's unlocked at level 5 at the same time as the Gyms become unlocked. Potions heal 20 HP of your Pokémon.

SUPER POTIONS

Once you reach Trainer level 10, Super Potions will become available to you. These are much better than Potions and heal 50 HP of your injured Pokémon.

You'll find plenty of Potions when you check in at PokéStops.

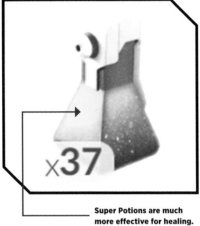

Super Potions are much more effective for healing.

EXPERT ADVICE

When your Trainer reaches level 10, and has access to Super Potions, you are very unlikely to use these regular weaker Potions. We recommend that you regularly delete them from your Bag, creating space for more useful items.

MAX POTIONS

The final health-restoring Potion is unlocked at Trainer Level 25. The Max Potion is the ultimate health Potion, completely restoring a Pokémon's HP.

Hyper Potions are essential items to carry.

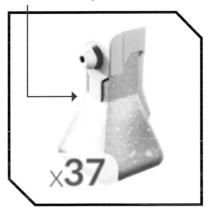

×37

HYPER POTIONS

Upon reaching Trainer level 15, you will be given access to the amazing Hyper Potions. Each Hyper Potion restores 200 HP to any of your battle-damaged Pokémon.

REVIVES

If your Pokémon has fainted during battle, then you'll need to revive it before it can be healed. Revives become available to you at Trainer level 5, and will restore your fainted Pokémon with half HP.

×36

Revive fallen Pokémon before healing them.

MAX REVIVE

Max Revive is the ultimate way to bring back your fainted Pokémon, but these are not available until you reach Trainer level 30. Use one of these amazing items to revive your fainted Pokémon with full HP.

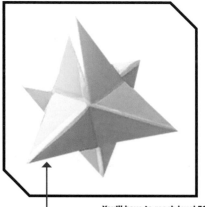

You'll have to reach level 30 to access Max Revive.

Visit PokéStops often to stock up on items.

London Victoria Station

EXPERT ADVICE

If you have run out of Revives or Max Revives, and need to bring back a fainted Pokémon, you can always power it up using Stardust and Candies. This will grant it a small HP boost, whilst reviving it at the same time.

POKÉSTOP RESTOCK

Once an item has been unlocked for use, it is then collectable from PokéStops when you visit. Make sure you visit often to collect plenty of free items and XP as well. Remember you can get a random number of items from each PokéStop. If you get three items, you will earn 50 XP, and if you get six items, you will earn 100 XP.

LEVEL UP RESTOCKS

Once an item has been unlocked, you will be rewarded with bonus items each time you level up. This is always a great bonus, and will always be collected even if it will overfill your bag. Take a look at the table opposite, which shows all the bonus items received for levelling up.

LEVEL UP REWARDS

Level	Experience required	Total experience	Item rewards	Item unlocks
2	1000	1000	PokéBall x10	
3	2000	3000	PokéBall x15	
4	3000	6000	PokéBall x15	
5	4000	10,000	PokéBall x20, Potion x10, Revive x10, Incense	Gyms, Potion, Revive
6	5000	15,000	PokéBall x15, Potion x10, Revive x5, Incubator	
7	6000	21,000	PokéBall x15, Potion x10, Revive x5, Incense	
8	7000	28,000	PokéBall x15, Potion x10, Revive x5, Razz Berry x10, Lure Module	Razz Berry
9	8000	36,000	PokéBall x15, Potion x10, Revive x5, Razz Berry x3, Lucky Egg	
10	9000	45,000	PokéBall x20, Super Potion x20, Revive x10, Razz Berry x10, Incense, Lucky Egg, Egg Incubator, Lure Module	Super Potion
11	10,000	55,000	PokéBall x15, Super Potion x 10, Revive x3, Razz Berry x 3	
12	10,000	65,000	Great Ball x20, Super Potion x10, Revive x3, Razz Berry x3	Great Ball
13	10,000	75,000	Great Ball x10, Super Potion x10, Revive x3, Razz Berry x3	
14	10,000	85,000	Great Ball x10, Super Potion x10, Revive x3, Razz Berry x3	
15	15,000	100,000	Great Ball x15, Hyper Potion x20, Revive x10, Razz Berry x10 Incense, Lucky Egg, Egg Incubator, Lure Module	Hyper Potion
16	20,000	120,000	Great Ball x10, Hyper Potion x10, Revive x5, Razz Berry x5	
17	20,000	140,000	Great Ball x10, Hyper Potion x10, Revive x5, Razz Berry x5	
18	20,000	160,000	Great Ball x10, Hyper Potion x10, Revive x5, Razz Berry x5	
19	25,000	185,000	Great Ball x15, Hyper Potion x10, Revive x5, Razz Berry x5	
20	25,000	210,000	Ultra Ball x20, Hyper Potion x20, Revive x20, Razz Berry x20, Incense x2, Lucky Egg x2, Egg Incubator x2, Lure Module x2	Ultra Ball
21	50,000	260,000	Ultra Ball x10, Hyper Potion x10, Revive x10, Razz Berry x10	
22	75,000	335,000	Ultra Ball x10, Hyper Potion x10, Revive x10, Razz Berry x10	
23	100,000	435,000	Ultra Ball x10, Hyper Potion x10, Revive x10, Razz Berry x10	
24	125,000	560,000	Ultra Ball x15, Hyper Potion x10, Revive x10, Razz Berry x10	
25	150,000	710,000	Ultra Ball x25, Max Potion x20, Revive x15, Razz Berry x15, Incense, Lucky Egg, Egg Incubator, Lure Module	Max Potion
26	190,000	900,000	Ultra Ball x10, Max Potion x15, Revive x10, Razz Berry x15	
27	200,000	1,100,000	Ultra Ball x10, Max Potion x15, Revive x10, Razz Berry x15	
28	250,000	1,350,000	Ultra Ball x10, Max Potion x15, Revive x10, Razz Berry x15	
29	300,000	1,650,000	Ultra Ball x10, Max Potion x15, Revive x10, Razz Berry x15	
30	350,000	2,000,000	Ultra Ball x30, Max Potion x20, Max Revive x20, Razz Berry x20, Incense x3, Lucky Egg x3, Egg Incubator x3, Lure Module x3	Max Revive
31	500,000	2,500,000	Ultra Ball x10, Max Potion x15, Max Revive x10, Razz Berry x15	
32	500,000	3,000,000	Ultra Ball x10, Max Potion x15, Max Revive x10, Razz Berry x15	
33	750,000	3,750,000	Ultra Ball x10, Max Potion x15, Max Revive x10, Razz Berry x15	
34	1,000,000	4,750,000	Ultra Ball x10, Max Potion x15, Max Revive x10, Razz Berry x15	
35	1,250,000	6,000,000	Ultra Ball x30, Max Potion x20, Max Revive x20, Razz Berry x20, Incense x2, Lucky Egg, Lure Module	
36	1,500,000	7,500,000	Ultra Ball x20, Max Potion x20, Max Revive x10, Razz Berry x20	
37	2,000,000	9,500,000	Ultra Ball x20, Max Potion x20, Max Revive x10, Razz Berry x20	
38	2,500,000	12,000,000	Ultra Ball x20, Max Potion x20, Max Revive x10, Razz Berry x20	
39	3,000,000	15,000,000	Ultra Ball x20, Max Potion x20, Max Revive x10, Razz Berry x20	
40	5,000,000	20,000,000	Ultra Ball x40, Max Potion x40, Max Revive x40, Razz Berry x40 Incense x4, Lucky Egg x4, Egg Incubator x4, Lure Module x4	

FINDING LOCAL GYMS AND POKÉSTOPS

LOCATIONS, LOCATIONS, LOCATIONS

GYMS

Pokémon Go Gyms are very tall buildings that can be seen for quite a distance on your in-game map. They usually have a Pokémon sitting proudly on top, which is the highest ranked Pokémon that has been left defending the Gym, and will be circled by a Red, Blue, or Yellow glow depending on the team that currently occupies the Gym. If you are having trouble finding a Gym, then read on as we reveal the best places to find them.

The taller a Gym is, the higher a level it's currently at.

TRAIN STATIONS

Nearly every train station we have ever visited is also a Pokémon Go Gym. If you travel by train a lot, this will give you plenty of opportunities to do some battling while you are waiting for your train, especially if you live in a country with trains that are regularly late! However, as many players use trains as a means of transport, these Gyms are usually pretty tough and can be very hard to keep control of for any sustained period of time.

Keep an eye out for Gyms located at local churches, train stations, and public buildings.

You can find all sorts of Gyms and PokéStops in your local area.

CHURCHES

Another popular spot to find Pokémon Go Gyms is at local churches. Again, nearly all places of worship are also Gyms, so there is guaranteed to be one fairly near to where you live. These are a little easier to beat than the Gyms found at train stations, although it is probably not a good idea to try defending them on a weekend when there are lots of weddings, and, of course, Sunday services going on. And of course, as always, be respectful when near a place of worship.

You can often see Gyms on the map from far away.

POKÉSTOPS

There are PokéStops dotted around everywhere, giving you plenty of access to additional gear and experience. PokéStops can be found at places of interest, and there are usually plenty in every town, village, and city. A simple walk around your local area will help you discover most of them, but they are usually found at local parks and play areas, museums, post offices, and other areas of public interest.

London Victoria Station

Spin the PokéStop to receive lots of goodies.

PUBS

Another popular venue for Pokémon Go Gyms are public houses. However, not all pubs are Gyms and many of them are actually PokéStops instead. If you can find a local pub that is a Gym, or a PokéStop, then that's a great way to spend a day! Always remember that you should never hang around a place of business without buying anything, and you can't go inside unless you're the legal age required in your country.

Travel around to find the best PokéStops.

USEFUL APPS

Pokémon Go has been very popular, and due to this popularity, many small developers have created apps to help you. While we do not recommend any of these apps, there are plenty of free apps available to help you if you are struggling to find Pokémon or Gyms.

EXPLORE

The best way to discover your local Gyms and PokéStops is to get out and explore. Whilst it is easy to find the station and church Gyms, there are often other notable buildings that have been designated as Pokémon Go Gyms. Try equipping an Incense and going for a walk around your local town or village, and make a note of all the Gyms in the area. Selecting the Gym will reveal its level, location, and also list all the Pokémon currently defending it. The higher the level of the Gym, the more Pokémon you will have to defeat in order to take control of it.

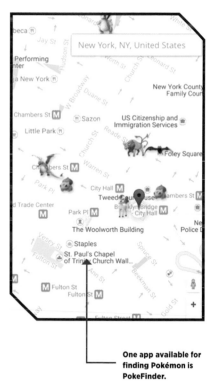

One app available for finding Pokémon is PokeFinder.

TRAINING

POWER UP YOUR GYMS

If your team is already in control of a Gym, you obviously can't battle it to take control, but instead you can battle it to train your Pokémon, earn experience, and increase the Gym's Prestige. This is really important for several reasons, and is actually really good battle practice.

Two Sculputers
Gym level 9

43225 / 50000

CarterrHO3

SNORLAX
CP 1663

CP 1181   CP 1098   CP 1023
Golduck   Vaporeon   Vaporeon

CP 987   CP 1023   CP 782
Electrode Pidgeot   Jolteon

HOW TO TRAIN

When entering a Gym owned by your team, rather than seeing the battle Gym symbol, you'll see a fight symbol instead. Simply click this and you can begin training your Pokémon. The entire training system operates exactly like a Gym battle. You can choose your team of six attackers to face the Pokémon currently occupying the Gym, and must face them one at a time in order. This was changed in an updated version of the game – previously you could only use one Pokémon, rather than a complete team of six.

You can now choose from a team of six Pokémon to battle with.

LEVEL ADJUSTED CP

In a recent update to Pokémon Go, training in Gyms was changed for the better. Now when you go training in a local Gym, all of the Pokémon you face will have their CP adjusted based on your current Trainer level. This is great news for lower level players, as it will offer them fair opportunity to practice and win, and help to increase the Gym's Prestige level.

EXPERT ADVICE

When battling in Gyms, try to save your Charge Attack moves for the right moment. Remember, you do not always have to use them the moment they are ready!

Lower level Trainers will now have better chances to practice at Gyms.

FIGHT

When training, the battle is exactly like a Gym battle. You attack and dodge exactly the same way. The only real difference is you are competing for experience, and to help power up the Gym rather than to take it over. Use these sessions to try out new Pokémon against others, and see which ones work best for you. This is a great way to decide on your staples for your main team.

Jolteon

782 Bulletproof70

Vaporeon

179 Ashwhite90

Super effective!

GO

Try training with a wide variety of Pokémon.

PUMP UP THE POWER

Every time you win a battle in the training arena, you will earn experience points and also Prestige points for the Gym. Every Gym starts at level 1 and slowly increases its Prestige, getting steadily harder to defeat the more effort you put into training. Once a Gym reaches level 10 it is impossible to increase its Prestige any further. Here is a table showing the Prestige needed to increase the Gym levels:

Gym Level	Total Prestige	Prestige	Defending Pokémon
1	0	0	1
2	2,000	2,000	2
3	4,000	4,000	3
4	8,000	4,000	4
5	12,000	4,000	5
6	16,000	4,000	6
7	20,000	10,000	7
8	30,000	10,000	8
9	40,000	10,000	9
10	50,000	MAX	10

EARN EXTRA PRESTIGE

The maximum amount of Prestige points available for each battle is 1000, and you also get 10 percent of this total as your personal XP. Using your best Pokémon will get you reasonable results, but you can earn extra Prestige by really challenging yourself in these battles, and using a Pokémon with vastly reduced CP compared to that of the defending Pokémon. This technique will enable you to power up the Gym much faster.

A fully levelled-up Gym has a maximum of 50,000 Prestige points.

Wesleyan Chapel
Gym level 10

P0k3mast3rDan

VAPOREON
CP 2449

This Gym is too far away

Electrode

88

CP 987

2

Slowbro

203

MULTIPLAYER TRAINING

Just like with Gym battles, you can also train with friends to level up the Gym faster. This works in exactly the same way as multiplayer Gym battles, only this time you are working together to earn experience and Prestige. Once again, working as a team, you can take down the defending Pokémon faster, whilst taking less damage and enabling you to level up the Gym more efficiently. When working together you also gain another defending Pokémon as soon as the Gym reaches level 2, making it slightly more difficult to take down quickly.

Work as a team to increase a Gym's Prestige.

THE ART OF DODGING

AVOID ATTACKS

When battling in a Gym, you'll need to be able to learn to dodge incoming attacks in order to survive longer in battles. Successfully dodging an attack can reduce the damage you take by up to 75 per cent, so perfecting this skill is a no-brainer if you want to become a master Gym battler.

HOW TO DODGE

In order to dodge an incoming attack, simply swipe your finger across the screen to the left or right just after the screen flashes yellow, and before the HP bar turns orange. The timing of this action must be perfect to complete the dodge and reduce the damage (you have roughly 0.7 second for a normal attack).

WHAT TO DODGE

Although all attacks can be dodged, it is best to watch carefully as you battle and ensure that you dodge your opponent's most powerful attacks. There are plenty of ways to tell when these are coming. Usually, there is an announcement and a longer than normal break between attack animations. At this point, stop attacking and keep your eyes fixed on the screen for a yellow flash.

Wait for the flashes before dodging.

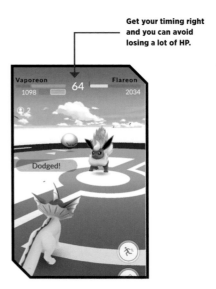

Get your timing right and you can avoid losing a lot of HP.

POKÉMON GO EXPERT BATTLE GUIDE

PERFECT TIMING

To help you understand all of the charge moves, we've compiled this handy chart providing all the vital information you'll need.

Name	Attack Type	Attack Power	Duration (ms*)	Dodge Window (ms*)	Critical Chance%	Energy Cost
Aerial Ace	Flying	30	2900	600	5%	25
Air Cutter	Flying	30	3300	900	25%	25
Ancient Power	Rock	35	3600	350	5%	25
Aqua Jet	Water	25	2350	400	5%	20
Aqua Tail	Water	45	2350	200	5%	50
Blizzard	Ice	100	3900	0	5%	100
Body Slam	Normal	40	1560	200	5%	50
Bone Club	Ground	25	1600	250	5%	25
Brick Break	Fighting	30	1600	400	25%	33
Brine	Water	25	2400	350	5%	25
Bubble Beam	Water	30	2900	200	5%	25
Bug Buzz	Bug	75	4250	1500	5%	50
Bulldoze	Ground	35	3400	1100	5%	25
Cross Chop	Fighting	60	2000	300	25%	100
Cross Poison	Poison	25	1500	300	25%	25
Dark Pulse	Dark	45	3500	1100	5%	33
Dazzling Gleam	Fairy	55	4200	800	5%	33
Dig	Ground	70	5800	400	5%	33
Disarming Voice	Fairy	25	3900	1800	5%	20
Discharge	Electric	35	2500	700	5%	33
Dragon Claw	Dragon	35	1500	200	25%	50
Dragon Pulse	Dragon	65	3600	1200	5%	50
Draining Kiss	Fairy	25	2800	100	5%	20
Drill Peck	Flying	40	2700	900	5%	33
Drill Run	Ground	50	3400	700	25%	33
Earthquake	Ground	100	4200	1950	5%	100
Fire Blast	Fire	100	4100	400	5%	100
Fire Punch	Fire	40	2800	510	5%	33
Flame Burst	Fire	30	2100	400	5%	25
Flame Charge	Fire	25	3100	200	5%	20
Flame Wheel	Fire	40	4600	500	5%	25
Flamethrower	Fire	55	2900	900	5%	50
Flash Cannon	Steel	60	3900	1100	5%	33
Giga Drain	Grass	35	3600	1150	5%	33
Gunk Shot	Poison	65	3000	400	5%	100
Heart Stamp	Psychic	20	2550	300	5%	25
Heat Wave	Fire	80	3800	400	5%	100
Horn Attack	Normal	25	2200	300	5%	25
Hurricane	Flying	80	3200	1770	5%	100
Hydro Pump	Water	90	3800	2100	5%	100
Hyper Beam	Normal	120	5000	800	5%	100
Hyper Fang	Normal	35	2100	300	5%	33
Ice Beam	Ice	65	3650	1350	5%	50
Ice Punch	Ice	45	3500	1100	5%	33
Icy Wind	Ice	25	3800	700	5%	20
Iron Head	Steel	30	2000	250	5%	33

*Millisecond.

Name	Attack Type	Attack Power	Duration (ms*)	Dodge Window (ms*)	Critical Chance%	Energy Cost
Leaf Blade	Grass	55	2800	1000	25%	50
Low Sweep	Fighting	30	2250	150	5%	25
Magnet Bomb	Steel	30	2800	550	5%	25
Mega Drain	Grass	15	3200	1200	5%	20
Megahorn	Bug	80	3200	300	5%	100
Moonblast	Fairy	85	4100	600	5%	100
Mud Bomb	Ground	30	2600	450	5%	25
Night Slash	Dark	30	2700	200	25%	25
Ominous Wind	Ghost	30	3100	250	5%	25
Parabolic Charge	Electric	15	2100	400	5%	20
Petal Blizzard	Grass	65	3200	1000	5%	50
Play Rough	Fairy	55	2900	1300	5%	50
Poison Fang	Poison	25	2400	200	5%	20
Power Gem	Rock	40	2900	800	5%	33
Power Whip	Grass	70	2800	1300	0%	100
Psybeam	Psychic	40	3800	1300	5%	25
Psychic	Psychic	55	2800	1200	5%	50
Psyshock	Psychic	40	2700	500	5%	33
Psystrike	Psychic	70	5100	900	5%	100
Rest	Normal	35	3100	1296	0%	33
Rock Slide	Rock	50	3200	1400	5%	33
Rock Tomb	Rock	30	3400	900	25%	25
Scald	Water	55	4000	2100	5%	33
Seed Bomb	Grass	40	2400	500	5%	33
Shadow Ball	Ghost	45	3080	300	5%	33
Shadow Punch	Ghost	20	2100	300	5%	25
Shadow Sneak	Ghost	15	3100	600	5%	20
Signal Beam	Bug	45	3100	1000	5%	33
Sludge	Poison	30	2600	500	5%	25
Sludge Bomb	Poison	55	2600	500	5%	50
Sludge Wave	Poison	70	3400	900	5%	100
Solar Beam	Grass	120	4900	1700	5%	100
Stomp	Normal	30	2100	700	5%	25
Stone Edge	Rock	80	3100	400	50%	100
Struggle	Normal	15	1695	700	0%	20
Submission	Fighting	30	2100	150	5%	33
Swift	Normal	30	3000	500	5%	25
Thunder	Electric	100	4300	1550	5%	100
Thunder Punch	Electric	40	2400	250	5%	33
Thunderbolt	Electric	55	2700	800	5%	50
Twister	Dragon	25	2700	1750	5%	20
Vice Grip	Normal	25	2100	250	5%	20
Water Pulse	Water	35	3300	1000	5%	25
Wrap	Normal	25	4000	600	5%	20
X-Scissor	Bug	35	2100	250	5%	33

*Millisecond.

SPECIAL CHALLENGES

Some attacks are particularly difficult to dodge, so a little more practice is required to perfect defending against them. Here's what to watch out for.

BUBBLE

Bubble is not a charge move, but can also be a little tricky to dodge. If you want to avoid this attack, watch for the flash just before the last of the bubbles makes contact with your Pokémon.

Practice your dodges to avoid getting hit.

BLIZZARD

Blizzard can be challenging to dodge, as the animation covers the yellow flash, making it hard to spot. However, focus your attention on the block of ice instead and time your dodge just as your Pokémon breaks free.

BODY SLAM

This attack is one of the most difficult to dodge, as the flash occurs right at the start of the animation. Get ready to dodge as soon as the announcement is made, or there is a slight change in the attack timings.

EARTHQUAKE

The Earthquake attack is tough to dodge, as the flash is covered by the ground shaking animation. Keep your eyes to the ground and dodge based on the move, and not the flash, for this tricky attack.

HEAT WAVE

The Heat Wave attack is rather tough to dodge, as the animation itself looks very much like the yellow flash. To dodge this attack successfully, be patient, as the actual flash comes right at the end of the wave.

After you dodge, you can then get a quick hit in.

YOUR FIRST GYM BATTLE

LET'S GET READY TO RUMBLE

BEFORE YOU START

Every Gym in Pokémon Go is different. They all have different prestige levels and are defended by different Pokémon. Before you even attempt to take on the Gym and start battling, you can have a look at what lies ahead. To begin with, it's probably a good idea to start with a low level Gym rather than trying to take on a level 9 or 10 prestige Gym, which will almost certainly end in failure. However, remember – practice makes perfect.

Try taking on a low-level Gym first.

EARN MORE XP

Pokémon Go likes to favour the underdog in all battles and you'll earn much more experience if you win the battle using a Pokémon that has considerably less CP than the defending Pokémon. Remember, you'll need to dodge lots and use good type advantages to win. Are you up for the challenge?

Try to choose a mixed Pokémon team.

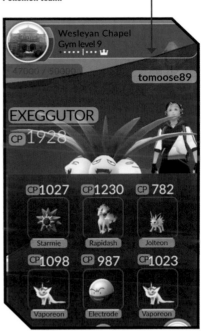

Your initial choice of Team is up to you.

CHOOSE YOUR POKÉMON

When taking on a Gym, you can select six of your Pokémon to battle for you in the arena. Before you start battling you can easily swap out Pokémon for any that are in your Bag. Just tap on the Pokémon you wish to change, and then select its replacement. Your Pokémon team is really important, as these are the ones on the frontline and will be taking and dishing out the damage. Be careful not to just choose your highest CP Pokémon, and instead look to choose a team that has great type match-ups against the Pokémon that are currently defending that Gym.

HOW TO ATTACK

The first thing you'll want to do is start attacking the defending Pokémon, and doing some damage to weaken it. Luckily, all you need to do to perform an attack is tap the screen anywhere, and your Pokémon will perform its basic attack. Keep tapping the screen and your Pokémon will keep performing its basic attack over and over again.

Power moves can cause a lot of damage.

Tap the screen to use basic attacks.

POWER MOVES

As the battle progresses, you'll notice that your energy bar increases, and once you have enough power you'll want to utilize your more powerful charge attack. These attacks do considerably more damage to the defending Pokémon, and can be the difference between winning and losing a battle. To perform your charge move, simply hold your finger on the screen, rather than tapping, and you should perform your Pokémon's power move.

Jolteon
CP 782
98
Flareon
2034

Dodging attacks can sometimes be the way to win battles.

DODGING ATTACKS

Another key to success in Gym battles is dodging your opponent's charge attacks. Dodging attacks is done by swiping your finger across the screen to the left or right just after the yellow flash, and before the damage bar turns orange. This can be a little tricky, but luckily we have devoted an entire section of this guide to help you perfect this. Turn to page 48 for some great tips on how to get better at dodging.

Starmie
CP1027
76
Hypno
1333

Hypno used Shadow Ball!

Press the switch button during battles to swap out Pokémon.

SWITCHING POKÉMON

If your Pokémon is running low on HP, you may want to switch it out before it faints. This can be done quickly and easily by pressing the switch button in the bottom right-hand corner of the screen. Remember, you will not be able to heal your Pokémon while you are in the Gym, so you will need to switch Pokémon quickly should you come up against a Pokémon that is strong against your current choice.

KNOCKED OUT POKÉMON

When a Pokémon is knocked out, it will instantly be replaced by the next Pokémon in your team, so you can continue with the battle. Pokémon never die, but after you have finished in the Gym you will need to remember to revive any Pokémon that have been knocked out and heal any that have taken serious damage, ready for the next battle.

Practice is the best way to improve.

Gengar   Exeggutor
CP964   1853
Bulletproof70   Worbletarn

GO

Starmie   73   Vaporeon
102?   1362

Keep an eye on your Pokémon's HP.

PRACTICE MAKES PERFECT

Don't worry if you don't get the hang of Gym battles straight away. There is plenty of time to practice and get better. It may take a few attempts to really understand your best Pokémon team, and also to get the hang of dodging attacks. You also might want to take a few turns just watching closely what happens in a battle, so you better understand the timings of thing. This will help you when you come to take on the harder Prestige Gyms.

SINGLE-PLAYER GYM BATTLES

TIME TO SHOW YOUR SKILLS

UNDERSTANDING GYM BATTLES

All Pokémon Gyms have a level, and understanding this will help you to determine which Gyms will be easiest tp take down on your own. The Gym's level is a reference to how many spaces there are for defending Pokémon. So a level 3 Gym has three defending Pokémon, while a level 9 Gym will have 9 defenders to battle through, and so on. All of the defending Pokémon will be from different Trainers.

A Gym's level determines how many defending Pokémon it has.

St Robert's Church
Gym level 3
•• ♛

6000 / 8000

legendevo86

PERSIAN
CP898

This Gym is too far away

GYM PRESTIGE

A Gym's Prestige is a measure of the Gym's popularity, and as its Prestige increases, so does its level. When training at a Gym that your team own, you can help to increase the Gym's Prestige, and if you raise the level enough, it will gain another defender spot in which you can add your own defender. Equally, by defeating a Gym owned by an opponent, you can reduce the Gym's Prestige and reduce the number of defending Pokémon. Once the number of defending Pokémon reaches zero, your team will then take control of the Gym.

Take down all of a Gym's defending Pokémon to claim it as your own.

1193 / 2000

L302408

FLAREON

CP 1821

This Gym is too far away

It's best to plan ahead before taking on any Gym battle.

William Whincup Memorial Gym level 1

PLAN YOUR ATTACK

Before stepping into the arena, take a long hard look at the defending Pokémon you are going to be facing, and choose a team of Pokémon to take them down as quickly as possible. To do this you will really need to know your type match-ups and learn very quickly how to identify each Pokémon's primary weakness.

KNOW YOUR STRENGTHS AND WEAKNESSES

Not only is the Pokémon's type important, but also its attack type. If an Electric-type Pokémon performs an Electric-type attack, it gains a Same Type Attack Bonus (STAB). This results in more damage, and considerably more damage when directed against a Pokémon that has weakness to that attack type.

Pokémon Type	Strong Against	Weak Against
Fire	Steel, Bug, Ice, Grass	Ground, Rock, Water
Water	Fire, Ground, Rock	Electric, Grass
Grass	Water, Ground, Rock	Flying, Poison, Bug, Fire, Ice
Electric	Water, Flying	Ground, Grass, Steel, Dragon
Psychic	Fighting, Poison	Bug, Ghost, Dark
Ground	Fire, Electric, Poison, Rock, Steel	Water, Grass, Ice
Poison	Grass, Fairy	Ground, Psychic
Fighting	Normal	Flying, Psychic, Fairy
Rock	Fire, Ice, Flying, Bug	Water, Grass, Fighting, Ground, Steel
Bug	Grass, Psychic, Dark	Flying, Fire, Rock
Fairy	Fighting, Dragon, Dark	Poison, Steel
Ghost	Psychic, Ghost	Ghost, Dark
Dragon	Dragon	Ice, Dragon, Fairy
Ice	Grass, Ground, Flying, Dragon	Fire, Fighting, Rock, Steel
Flying	Grass, Fighting, Bug	Electric, Ice, Rock
Steel	Fairy, Ice, Rock	Fighting, Fire, Ground
Normal	None	Fighting
Dark	Psychic, Ghost	Fighting, Fairy, Bug

For a more specific list of each Pokémon's strengths and weaknesses, check the Poképrofiles section on page 104.

LESS EFFECTIVE ATTACKS

In the GBA/DS/3DS Pokémon games, some Pokémon types are immune to attacks from certain types. This has not been included in Pokémon go, but instead some attacks are less effective against some types of Pokémon. To help you effectively pair Pokémon in battles, we have compiled a list of these less effective Pokémon.

Choosing the right type of Pokémon for battles is essential.

Pokémon Type	Less Effective Against
Electric	Ground
Dragon	Fairy
Fighting	Ghost
Normal	Ghost
Ground	Flying
Psychic	Dark
Poison	Steel

Super-effective
attacks will cause
lots of damage.

ONE AT A TIME

Taking on Gyms need not be a trial, although it may seem that way sometimes, particularly when taking on a high-Prestige Gym. Remember to take each Battle one at a time, focus on dodging the charge attacks, and do as much damage as you can as quickly as possible. Remember to switch out heavily damaged Pokémon before they faint, and don't worry if it takes you a few attempts. Before long you'll be the king of the ring!

A Golduck is highly
effective against all
sorts of Pokémon.

TIME LIMITS

Be careful not to take too long on each battle, as there is a strict time limit. This is really important, because if you take too long the battle will end, and you will be thrown out of the Gym. You have exactly 100 seconds for each battle, so attack fast and don't waste any time.

Keep an eye out for the time when entering into Gym battles.

If you don't defeat your opponent within the time limit, you'll be thrown out of the Gym.

TAKE CONTROL

Once you have defeated all the Pokémon at the Gym, you will reduce the Prestige level and knock one of the defenders off the stack. Repeat the process until all the defenders are gone, and the Gym will be yours for the taking. You can now leave a Pokémon at the Gym to defend it for you. Turn to page 76 for some guidance on the best Pokémon to choose to defend a Gym for you.

YOU WIN!

Wings and Ropes
Gym level 2

Gym Prestige
3936 / 4000

+350
3

Pokemon Defeated:
☆ ☆ ☆

Reduce a Gym's
Prestige level to zero
to win it for your Team.

Claim a Gym, and you'll
be able to get all sorts
of cool rewards.

MULTI-PLAYER GYM BATTLES

DOUBLE TROUBLE

Higher level Prestige Gyms can be a real chore to take down on your own, but luckily others can lend a hand, and you can work together to topple the tower. Teaming up with other members of your team is really the only way to take control of level 10 Gyms. As Gyms only decrease one level at a time and one defender at a time, the level 10 Gyms would never fall without multi-player attacks.

THE BATTLE

Both players battle the same Pokémon at the same time, making the fight much faster and easier for both players. If you work together you can get through even the toughest of the defending Pokémon, and start dropping the levels rapidly. Remember to dodge plenty, just like when taking on the Gyms on your own.

Two players working together are much more effective when taking down a Gym.

Jolteon
CP 782
97
Flareon
2034

You can even join forces with a trainer from a rival Team to beat Gyms.

RUSSIAN ROULETTE

It is also possible to take on Gym with a player from a rival team. You still get to fight together and help each other out during the battle to take over the Gym. Once the fight is over and the Gym is defeated, it then becomes a battle to place a defender in the Gym first, before the player from the other team can do so. They can, of course, battle you to take you out, but it is still quite fun.

SELECTING BEST ATTACKERS

THE POKÉMON ELITE

Some Pokémon are naturally better at attacking than others, while some are just good all-rounders. Obviously you are limited to the Pokémon you have managed to catch and evolve, but you should always be aware of the best options available to you so you can try to catch them and become a Pokémon master. Let's take a look at the best attacking monsters in the game.

LAPRAS

Type   Ice/Water
Max CP   2980
Best Moves: Frost Breath
                 Blizzard

Lapras is possibly the best attacker in the game, with elite stats and powerful Ice STAB moves. There is simply no better Pokémon in the game for taking down a Dragonite. Lapras also performs well against many other popular defenders, including Grass-type Pokémon, so if you have one, this should be the first Pokémon added to your Gym attacking team.

Take on a Gym with a Lapras, and you've got a great chance of winning.

SNORLAX

Type	Normal
Max CP	3112
Best Moves:	Lick
	Hyper Beam/
	Body Slam

Snorlax is a behemoth in Pokémon Go at both attacking and defending, due to it having no major weaknesses. Snorlax can battle against anything without fear, making it an obvious choice for your team if you have one that is not currently being use to protect a Gym.

CP 1104

Snorlax

HP 156/156

Normal	422.21 kg	2.08 m
Type	Weight	Height

110
STARDUST

10
SNORLAX CANDY

POWER UP   1300   2

Snorlax is an all-round attacker and defender.

You'll often see Dragonites at the top of Gyms.

CP 1127

Dragonite ✏

HP 84 / 84

Dragon / Flying	383.32 kg XL	2.8 m XL
Type	Weight	Height

🔋 8717
STARDUST

🍬 0
DRATINI CANDY

POWER UP   🔋 1300   🍬 2

ARCANINE

Type   Fire
Max CP   2983
Best Moves: Fire Fang/Bite
                  Fire Blast

Arcanine has the highest attack stats of any Fire-type Pokémon in the game, making it the obvious choice for any Gym with Grass-type Pokémon in residence. It can also perform well in other battles, as long as it doesn't involve Water-type Pokémon. Avoid this weakness and Arcanine is a force to be reckoned with.

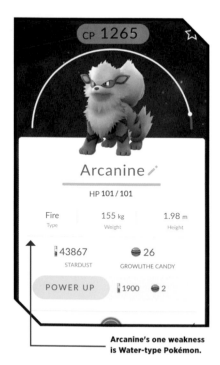

CP 1265

Arcanine ✏

HP 101 / 101

Fire	155 kg	1.98 m
Type	Weight	Height

🔋 43867
STARDUST

🍬 26
GROWLITHE CANDY

POWER UP   🔋 1900   🍬 2

Arcanine's one weakness is Water-type Pokémon.

DRAGONITE

Type   Dragon/Flying
Max CP   3500
Best Moves: Dragon Breath
                  Dragon Claw

With the best overall stats in the game, Dragonite is always going to feature highly on every list, and it is very useful as an attacker, as well as being an exceptional defender. Dragonite has resistance to Fire-, Water-, and Grass-type Pokémon, so can be a great choice for defeating many of the top choice defenders in a Gym.

POKÉMON GO EXPERT BATTLE GUIDE

ALAKAZAM

Type   Psychic
Max CP   1813
Best Moves: Psycho Cut
               Psychic

Alakazam is a beast of a Psychic Pokémon that benefits from STAB damage on Psychic-type moves. If you have managed to train a decent Alakazam, it is definitely a contender for your attacking team. It can perform well against almost all Pokémon.

Take on all Water-type Pokémon with Victreebel.

Alakazam benefits from strong Psychic moves.

VICTREEBEL

Type   Grass/Poison
Max CP   2530
Best Moves: Razor Leaf
               Solar Beam/Leaf Blade

Victreebel is quite possibly the best Grass-type Pokémon available in the game for shooting down all the Water-type Pokémon that are often seen defending Gyms. With great attacks, Victreebel can take them down quickly, but you'll need to dodge well as it does not have very good defensive stats.

A common sight at Gyms, Vaporeon is a solid choice.

EXEGGUTOR
Type   Grass/Psychic
Max CP   2955
Best Moves: Zen Headbutt
              Solar Beam

Exeggutor is a good addition to any attacking team, and is great for taking down any Water-, Ground-, or Rock-type Pokémon. If you are practiced at dodging, Exeggutor is an absolute gem of a team member, and could end up being one of the first Pokémon on your team sheet.

VAPOREON
Type   Water
Max CP   2816
Best Moves: Water Gun
              Hydro Pump/Aqua Tail

Vaporeon is one of the most commonly available attackers in the game, with good stats and great attacks. It's a good all-round Pokémon for both attacking and defending, and should definitely be considered for your attacking team.

Exeggutor can take down many different types.

SLOWBRO

Type   Psychic/Water
Max CP   2597
Best Moves: Water Gun
            Psychic

Slowbro is another strong attacker that can perform well in a number of different match-ups. Fire-, Ground-, and Rock-type Pokémon will get torn to shreds by Slowbro, but it can also be a rather handy utility attacker for taking down other stubborn defenders. Slowbro is a definite contender.

Starmie is another good all-round attacker and defender.

An often underrated Pokémon that can suprise Trainers.

STARMIE

Type   Psychic/Water
Max CP   2182
Best Moves: Water Gun
            Hydro Pump/Psychic

Starmie is not an obvious choice as an attacker, but we have found that it is really versatile, and can perform really well. Its stats are reasonable, and it does well in most battles, except against Grass-type Pokémon. Remember to dodge lots, and Starmie could be the star of your team.

Sandslash is able to stand up to Poison-type attacks.

VENUSAUR

Type Grass/Poison
Max CP 2580
Best Moves: Vine Whip
Solar Beam/Petal Blizzard

Venusaur may not be in the elite tier, but is definitely a good attack option, particularly as many of the Gyms seem to favour Water-type Pokémon as defenders. Although not quite as good as Victreebel and Exeggcutor, Venusaur is still a good Grass type Pokémon, and a worthy addition to your team, particularly if you don't have another decent Grass-type attacker.

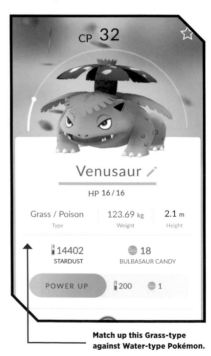

SANDSLASH

Type Ground
Max CP 1810
Best Moves: Mud Shot
Earthquake

Sandslash is a great attacker, if the Gym you are facing features Poison-type Pokémon. Sandslash has resistance to Poison-type moves, and therefore will help make those battles easy. It is wise to have a decent Sandslash or Golem available as an attack option should you ever need it.

Match up this Grass-type against Water-type Pokémon.

HYPNO

Type   Psychic
Max CP 2184
Best Moves: Zen Headbutt
              Psychic

Hypno is one Pokémon we are sure you will have, and it makes a good choice for your attacking team. It is a good all-round Pokémon for most match-ups, and can perform well in almost any battle. If you have a spare slot in your team's roster, then Hypno could be a good addition.

Lickitung is a good low DP attacker to select.

CP 332

Lickitung ✏

HP 68 / 68

Normal	70.04 kg	1.04 m
Type	Weight	Height

🏺 110   ⚪ 15
STARDUST   LICKITUNG CANDY

POWER UP   🏺 800   ⚪ 1

CP 917

Hypno ✏

HP 95 / 95

Psychic	27.88 kg	1.36 m
Type	Weight	Height

🏺 61379   ⚪ 122
STARDUST   DROWZEE CANDY

POWER UP   🏺 1900   ⚪ 2

15

Not an obvious choice, but Hypno is a good all-rounder.

PRESTIGE ATTACKERS

Whist it's a good idea to power up your attacking team as much as possible, it is also good to have a team of low DP attackers to help Prestige Gyms quicker. For this you'll need at least five Pokémon with a CP of under 750. Likely candidates are Sandslash, Marowak, Starmie, Slowbro, Exeggutor, Hypno, Arcanine, Ivysaur, Weepinbell, Tangela, Lickitung, Clefable, and Wigglytuff.

SELECTING BEST DEFENDERS

HOLDING YOUR TERRITORY

Once you have taken control of the Gym, you can select one of your Pokémon from your storage to defend the Gym on your behalf. Not all Pokémon are equal, and making the right choice will earn you 10 PokéCoins, and 500 Stardust every 21 hours. With so many Pokémon to choose from, it can be tough to make the right choice. To help you make a decision, here are our top contenders.

SNORLAX

Type	Normal
Max CP	3112
Best Moves:	Zen Headbutt, Earthquake/
	Hyper Beam/Body Slam

Snorlax is without doubt the best defender available in Pokémon Go. No other Pokémon is able to get one over on Snorlax, and it has two good attacks, making it a great choice as an attacker too.

LAPRAS

Type	Ice/Water
Max CP	2980
Best Moves:	Ice Shard,
	Blizzard/Ice Beam

Lapras is another great choice as a defender. It has very strong stats and very powerful STAB (same-type attack bonus) moves that can do plenty of damage. The Ice Shard attack is great as a basic defensive move, and Blizzard can be really tricky to dodge.

CP **1104**

Snorlax

HP 156 / 156

Normal	422.21 kg	2.08 m
Type	Weight	Height

110 STARDUST

10 SNORLAX CANDY

POWER UP   1300   2

A Gym defended by Snorlax is tough to beat.

Sparky   95   Lapras
CP 1008   868

3

Super effective!

Use the Ice Shard move to repel attacking Pokémon.

Dragonites are hard to beat at any Gym.

You won't see many of these defending a Gym.

DRAGONITE

Type Dragon/Flying
Max CP 3500
Best Moves: Steel Wing
Dragon Pulse

Dragonite boasts the highest base stats in the game at the moment, and is perfect for both attacking and defending. Dragonite is resistant to Fire-, Water-, and Grass-type Pokémon, making it a tough opponent for many of the common attackers.

ALAKAZAM

Type Psychic
Max CP 1813
Best Moves: Confusion
Psychic

Alakazam is a tough Pokémon to raise, and not many are lucky enough to have one in their ranks. However, if you do, he is a real tough cookie, and can be great for holding down a Gym. Alakazam's Psychic STAB moves make him a good attacker too.

SLOWBRO

Type   Psychic/Water
Max CP   2597
Best Moves: Confusion
            Psychic

Slowbro has very good stats, and is another Pokémon that is good at both attacking and defending. It's Confusion and Psychic attack combo is the best defensive move pairing in the game and, when combined with a Psychic STAB bonus, it's easy to see why Slowbro is a popular choice.

POLIWRATH

Type   Fighting/Water
Max CP   2505
Best Moves: Bubble Ice Punch/
            Hydro Pump/Submission

Poliwrath is one of the very best Pokémon for defensive stats and a really good choice, providing it has the Bubble attack. This basic attack can be tough to dodge, making it a tricky opponent in any Gym.

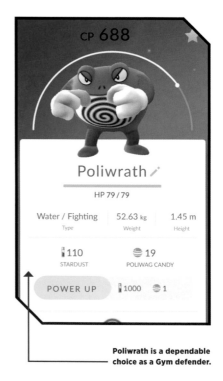

Psychic and Confusion moves are Slowbro's trademarks.

Poliwrath is a dependable choice as a Gym defender.

With solid stats, Wigglytuff is a very good option.

Many Gyms are defended by multiple Vaporeon.

WIGGLYTUFF
Type   Fairy/Normal
Max CP   2177
Best Moves: Pound
              Play Rough

Wigglytuff is a great choice as a defender. It has good stats and no real weakness to any of the major attacking threats. The only Pokémon that can cause problems for Wigglytuff are Nidoqueen and Muk, and neither are used that much.

VAPOREON
Type   Water
Max CP   2816
Best Moves: Water Gun
              Water Pulse

Almost everybody has at least one Vaporeon, but that's not why it's a good choice as a defender. It has solid stats, high HP, and has two strong attacks. Nearly every Gym has a Vaporeon in it for a reason.

EXEGGUTOR

Type   Grass/Psychic
Max CP   2955
Best Moves: Confusion
             Psychic

Exeggutor is another key player in Pokémon Go, whether being used for attacking or defending. When defending, Exeggutor also has the best defensive move, and gains the STAB bonus like Slowbro. His weakness to Arcanine lets him down a little, though.

GOLDUCK

Type   Water
Max CP   2386
Best Moves: Confusion
             Ice Beam

While not the best defender, Golduck is a good choice, and fairly easy to get for most players. Not as tough as Vaporeon, Golduck has decent stats, and is only weak to Grass-types.

Exeggutor has one of the best defensive moves.

Golduck is often chosen as a solid Gym defender.

CLEFABLE

Type   Fairy
Max CP   2397
Best Moves: Zen Headbutt
             Dazzling Gleam

Clefable is a good solid choice as a defender, and performs very well in most situations. While not quite as good as Wigglytuff, Clefable is great against most common attackers and a very solid choice if you have one available in your roster.

OMASTAR

Type   Rock/Water
Max CP   2233
Best Moves: Rock Throw
             Rock Slide

Omastar is not an obvious choice for a defender and can be quite tough to catch, but has reasonable stats, and can be tough to take down. While it does suffer from weakness to Grass-type Pokémon, it can still be a serious contender in many battles.

Try mixing up a variety of Pokémon Gym defenders.

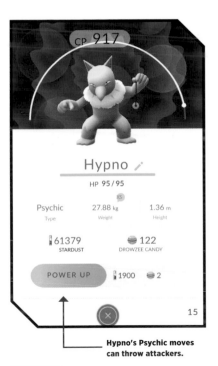

Hypno's Psychic moves can throw attackers.

HYPNO

Type   Psychic
Max CP   2184
Best Moves: Confusion
             Psychic

Not the strongest defender in the game, Hypno is commonly found and can be quite a pest to take down, making him an obvious choice if there are already other strong Pokémon in residence.

THE OTHERS

There are many other Pokémon that can make reasonable defenders, depending on the Pokémon already in residence in a Gym. It also totally depends on what Pokémon you have available to you and what Pokémon are commonly available as attackers in your local area. Remember, once you leave a Pokémon in a Gym, you are unable to power it up or do anything with it until the Gym has been defeated, and it is returned to your storage.

DEFEATING HARD POKÉMON

MAKE WINNING A HABIT

Completing your collection of Pokémon and filling up your Pokédex is only one part of the game. To become a true Pokémon Master, you're going to have to start battling in Gyms and making sure you win all of your fights. In this section of the Guide, we're going to be giving you expert tips and advice on how to do just that...

Mastering the dodge move is a key tactic.

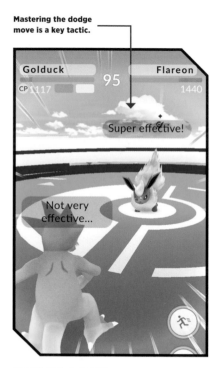

Snorlax are very tough foes to beat.

DODGE A LOT

Dodging attacks is without doubt the key to become a master of Gym battles. It is possible to take down huge CP Pokémon using Pokémon with only half their CP or less, if you can dodge well. In fact with enough practise and a little bit of luck, you can even get through an entire battle without taking a single hit. Remember, watch for the yellow flash!

DEFEATING SNORLAX

Snorlax is arguably the best defender in the whole game. He has good stats and favourable match-ups against almost all other Pokémon. To win this battle you'll need to time your dodges well and look out for Snorlax's hefty Body Slam charge move, which can be tough to dodge. Don't use your best Pokémon for this battle!

This rare Pokémon is a great Gym defender.

Crookisnab House
Gym level 2

Kkyyii

LAPRAS
CP 1805

This Gym is too far away

Taking down a high CP Dragonite isn't easy.

Former St. Lukes Church
Gym level 8

RPorter27

DRAGONITE
CP 2589

This Gym is too far away

DEFEATING LAPRAS

Lapras is another tough defender and is rather rare. Lapras has elite base stats and favourable match-ups against a huge array of popular attacking Pokémon, making it a great choice as a defender if you have one. Its Water-/Ice-type combo is powerful, and its Ice moves help protect it from Water-type weakness. Your best choice of attacker to defeat Lapras is Arcanine. While not always super effective, Arcanine has the power to do well against Lapras, and should win this battle fairly comfortably.

DEFEATING DRAGONITE

Dragonite is one of the most popular defenders and has the highest base stats of any Pokémon available in the game. It can reach ridiculously high CP levels if trained correctly, making Dragonite extremely popular at a lot of Gyms. Dragonite is resistant to Fire-, Water-, and Grass-type Pokémon, which covers a great deal of the most commonly used attackers. To defeat Dragonite, it's best to use Pokémon with Ice-type moves. So Lapras, Dewgong, and Cloyster should be able to take down this monster. Another thing to watch for with Dragonite is its charge moves. Each of Dragonite's three charge moves have very different timings. Watch carefully for the yellow flash and make sure you are ready to dodge.

Another challenging Pokémon to beat.

Slowbro will make short work of this Golduck.

DEFEATING ALAKAZAM

Alakazam is a rare sight, but does make a great defender, and can be tough to take down. If you can imagine a Hypno with more power HP and CP and better attacks... that's Alakazam. This could be a tough battle, but your best bet is either Gengar with Ghost-type moves or Hypno using Psychic-type moves. Whichever Pokémon you decide to use, the key to winning this battle will be dodging Alakazam's attacks.

DEFEATING SLOWBRO

Slowbro is a great defender, as it has resistance to Fire- and Water-types, plus does extra STAB damage on Psychic-type moves. Its base stats are usually very good, and it performs particularly well against Vaporeon. Although Slowbro does have type disadvantages against Bug-, Electric-, Dark-, and Ghost-type Pokémon, a lack of elite attacker of these types makes it a strong defender. The best choice to take down a Slowbro is an Exeggutor with the Solar Beam or Seed Bomb attack.

POKÉMON GO EXPERT BATTLE GUIDE

DEFEATING EXEGGUTOR

Another popular defender is Exeggutor, although it does not have the best stats. This Pokémon is the best Pokémon for attacking and defending against Vaporeon, whether it has Grass-type moves or not. It does hold its own against most attackers, and can cause great STAB damage with Psychic-type moves. Your best choice to defeat Exeggutor is Arcanine, particularly ones that boast the Seed Bomb or Solar Beam moves.

DEFEATING POLIWRATH

Poliwrath is a great Pokémon for both attacking and defending, and has great match-ups against many of the best Pokémon in the game. Its fighting type provides helpful resistance to rock type Pokémon, and its Bubble Attack can be really tricky to dodge. For the best results against Poliwrath, you should use big Grass-type Pokémon like Venusaur or Exeggutor. However, be careful, as some Poliwraths have the Ice Punch charge move, which can really help them in these battles.

You'll see many Vaporeon at Gyms.

An unusually tough Pokémon to beat.

DEFEATING VAPOREON

Vaporeon is easily one of the most common defenders in the game, due to how easy it is to catch and train them. Vaporeon has elite base stats, particularly defence, and performs well against most Pokémon including itself. This is why you will nearly always find a Vaporeon defending a Gym. The best choice for taking down a Vaporeon is a strong grass type Pokémon, like Exeggutor or Venusaur. Dragonite is great for taking out Vaporeon, and also Vileplume and Victreebel have favourable match-ups.

DEFEATING WIGGLYTUFF

Wigglytuff is an excellent choice as a defender, as it is almost impossible to exploit with an elite attacker. Just like Snorlax, it can be tough to take down and usually has pretty good stats, and a high HP. The best choices to take down Wigglytuff are Nidoqueen and Muk, although neither of these will be an easy battle to win.

Use Grass-type Pokémon in Omastar battles.

CP 758

Omastar ✎

HP 71 / 71

Rock / Water	109.63 kg	1.88 m
Type	Weight	Height

⚡41591   🍬 22
                SQUIRTLE CANDY

POWER UP   ⚡1300   🍬 2

Venusaur are weak against Fire-types.

ODEON Cinema
Gym level 3

Bd75sy

VENUSAUR
CP 1853

This Gym is too far away

DEFEATING OMASTAR

Omastar has great match-ups against many of the elite attacking Pokémon, which makes it a great choice as a defender. It can counter both Lapras and Dragonite, plus is resistant to Fire-type Pokémon. Its Rock Slide move has a low energy requirement and takes a while to perform, enabling Omastar to perform it almost non-stop during a battle. The best choices to use against Omastar are your big hitting Grass-type Pokémon – Exeggutor, Venusaur, Vileplume, and Victreebel.

DEFEATING VENUSAUR

Venusaur is another popular choice as a defending Pokémon, although not one that you see very often. It is great against Water-type Pokémon like Vaporeon, and also good against Rock/Ground-types like Golem and Rhydon. Whilst Venusaur is weak to Fire-types, it can usually hold up fairly well to Flareon. For the best results against Venusaur, try using Dragonite, Charizard, Arcanine, and Lapras.

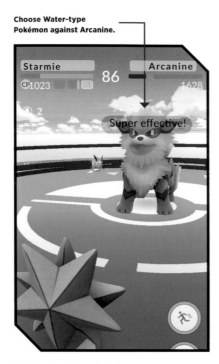

Choose Water-type Pokémon against Arcanine.

Starmie

CP1023

86

Arcanine

1628

2

Super effective!

Another strong choice to defend your Gyms.

ODEON Cinema
Gym level 3

L1771e

HYPNO
CP1590

This Gym is too far away

DEFEATING ARCANINE

Arcanine may not be the best defender in the game, but has elite base stats and a huge attack value. It will destroy any Grass-type Pokémon, but is easily taken down by almost any of the easily available Water-type Pokémon in the game. Your best choices for taking down an Arcanine are Vaporeon, Blastoise, Slowbro, Golduck, and Omastar. Other Pokémon like Rhydon, Golem and can also do well against Arcanine, giving you plenty of options.

DEFEATING HYPNO

Despite being commonly available to most players, Hypno is actually a good choice as a Gym defender, as it has no attackers that can perform super effective attacks against it. Whilst its stats are not great, it does perform rather well in most battles, and can be tricky to defeat. You are likely to encounter a high number of Hypnos in local Gyms, so learning how to take down this beast will be crucial in becoming a Gym master. For the best results, use either a Gengar with strong Ghost type moves or a stronger Hypno, and be prepared to dodge plenty.

Fire-types will help
defeat Victreebel.

Clefable are extremely
strong Gym defenders.

DEFEATING VICTREEBEL

Victreebel is very similar to Venusaur, only with slightly weaker stats. Again, its weakness to Fire-type Pokémon will mean you will not see too many occupying local Gyms, but that does not make it any less formidable. Victreebel has great match-ups against any Water-type Pokémon, and can even hold its own against Flareon. For the best results against Victreebel, try using Charizard, Dragonite, Arcanine, and Lapras.

DEFEATING CLEFABLE

Clefable is another strong choice as a Gym defender, and similar to Snorlax and Wigglytuff its type leaves it without any major weaknesses. While defending, its Dazzling Gleam attack has a long cooldown and low energy cost, enabling Clefable to keep using the attack over and over again. Clefable is great against Dragonite, so don't get the big guy out anywhere near this battle – instead use Muk, Weezing, or your strongest Poison-type Pokémon.

DEFEATING CHARIZARD

Charizard has reasonable stats and fairly high CP, making it an ominous defender. However, its weakness to Water-type Pokémon makes this a fairly easy battle. Use Vaporeon, Blastoise, Slowbro, Golduck, and Omastar for best results. Rhydon, Golem, and Poliwrath are also good choices for this battle.

Try using Fire-type Pokémon against Vileplume.

CP 516

Vileplume ✏

HP 58 / 58

Grass / Poison	15.04 kg	1.18 m
Type	Weight	Height

📊 606
STARDUST

🍬 37
ODDISH CANDY

POWER UP 📊 800 🍬 1

Charizard is vulnerable to Water-type attacks.

CP 883

Charizard ✏

HP 80 / 80

Fire / Flying	125.8 kg	1.48 m
Type	Weight	Height

📊 3261
STARDUST

🍬 25
CHARMANDER CANDY

POWER UP 📊 1600 🍬 2

DEFEATING VILEPLUME

Vileplume is another reasonable defender, but with weaker stats than Victreebel and Venusaur. Being a Grass-type Pokémon, Vileplume also shares their weakness to Fire Pokémon. However, it does perform very well against Vaporeon and other Water-type Pokémon, and can hold its own against Flareon. Good choices against Vileplume are Charizard, Dragonite, Arcanine, and Lapras.

DEFEATING MUK

Muk is not a defender you see very often, but it does have reasonable stats, and is worthy of a mention. Being a stage 2 Pokémon, its CP and HP are not huge, but it can perform well in some Gyms to back up other Pokémon. The best Pokémon to try using against Muk is Golem, but most Ground-type Pokémon have a serious type advantage in this battle.

DEFEATING GOLDUCK

Golduck is another Pokémon that has reasonable stats for stage 2 Pokémon. Its low CP and HP won't make it a popular choice, so it's unlikely you'll face too many of these. The best choice for taking down a Golduck is a strong Grass-type Pokémon like Exeggutor or Venusaur. Dragonite, Vileplume, and Victreebel will also perform well.

They may be big, but Gyarados aren't always that tough.

CP **1462**

Gyarados

HP 119 / 119

Water / Flying	235kg	7.6 m
Type	Weight	Height

📊 18977	🍬 16
STARDUST	MAGIKARP CANDY

POWER UP | 📊 2500 | 🍬 2

Ground-type Pokémon work well against Nidoking.

Exeggutor   Nidoking
CP 1637   **98**   1233

DEFEATING GYARADOS

There are a number of Gyms featuring Gyarados as a defender, and while they do have reasonable stats, they are not always that tough. Sometimes players may drop a Gyarados with the weaker Twister attacker as a defender, having already used a lot of their better one already. Your best choices for taking down Gyarados are Dragonite and Magneton. Raichu, Jolteon, and Electrode will also do fairly well, but do not have any resistance.

DEFEATING NIDOKING/ NIDOQUEEN

Nidoking and Nidoqueen is a rare sight in a Gym, but are still a reasonable defenders and thus worth a mention. Being a stage 3 Pokémon, they can reach quite a high CP and HP, and have reasonably good stats. The best choice to take down this pair is Sandslash, as its Ground-type reduces damage from Poison attacks. Other Pokémon that can do well against Nidoking and Nidoqueen include Marowak, Vaporeon, Alakazam, and Lapras.

ADVANCED SKILLS

TACTICS TO HELP YOU WIN MORE OFTEN

OTHER MEDALS

There are a number of other medals available in Pokémon Go, but these do not feature any Catch Bonuses. Here is the complete list:

Medal	Activity	Bronze	Silver	Gold
Backpacker	Visit PokéStops	100	1,000	2,000
Jogger	Walk long distances	10 km	100 km	1,000 km
Kanto	Register Pokémon in the Pokédex	20	50	100
Collector	Capture Pokémon	30	500	2,000
Scientist	Evolve Pokémon	3	20	200
Breeder	Hatch Eggs	10	100	1,000
Fisherman	Capture big Magikarp	3	50	300
Battle Girl	Win Gym battles	10	1000	1,000
Youngster	Catch tiny Rattata	3	50	300
Ace Trainer	Train at Gyms	10	100	1,000
Pikachu	Catch Pikachu	3	50	200

MAKE SPACE

There is nothing more frustrating than spinning a PokéStop and being told that your Bag is full, so that you get no reward. Although you can purchase Bag Upgrades (and this is a great way to add some more storage), it is best to do this a little later after you have obtained PokéCoins by defending multiple Gyms. To begin with, try deleting all your Potions, as once you get Super and Hyper Potions, you will not need them at all. This will instantly free up more space for more PokéBalls.

Make sure you have enough storage space when visiting PokéStops.

EASIER CAPTURES

While it can be a lot of fun capturing Pokémon in our environment, it is actually much easier to catch Pokémon when you turn the AR (augmented reality) off. The Pokémon will stop moving around, making them much easier to catch.

Turn AR off for easier Pokémon captures.

CHOOSE YOUR EEVEELUTION

One of the hidden hacks in Pokémon Go is a way to choose the form your Eevee will take when you evolve it. This is done by renaming your Eevee as one of the Eevee brothers from the Pokémon Anime as Pyro, Sparky, or Rainer. However, this will only work once for each form so choose carefully:

Eevee Name	Evolution
Pyro	Flareon
Sparky	Jolteon
Rainer	Vaporeon

GYM REWARDS

TIME TO CASH IN

COLLECT YOUR WINNINGS

If your Pokémon remains in place at a Gym for 21 hours, it will earn you a reward. Simply go to the PokéShop and click on the shield icon to collect your 10 PokéCoins and 500 Stardust. There are plenty of things to spend your coins on, and Stardust becomes really important for powering up your Pokémon.

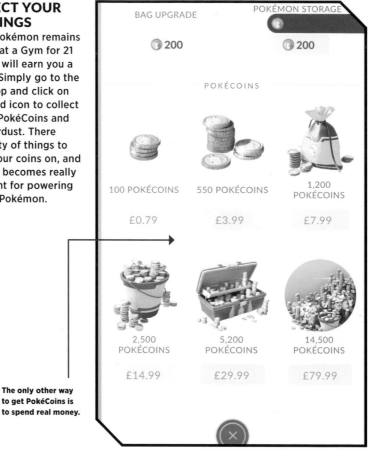

BAG UPGRADE

POKÉMON STORAGE

200

200

POKÉCOINS

100 POKÉCOINS

£0.79

550 POKÉCOINS

£3.99

1,200 POKÉCOINS

£7.99

2,500 POKÉCOINS

£14.99

5,200 POKÉCOINS

£29.99

14,500 POKÉCOINS

£79.99

The only other way to get PokéCoins is to spend real money.

MAXIMIZE REWARDS

You can hold as many Gyms as you wish at any one time, but the maximum payout you can receive is 100 PokéCoins and 5000 Stardust. If you live in an area where the Gym turnover rate is high, then it may be a good idea to try and place Pokémon at more Gyms giving you more chances to still be holding 10 when the timer expires.

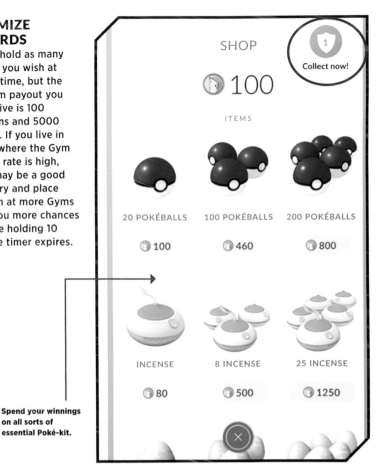

SHOP

🪙 100

ITEMS

20 POKÉBALLS	100 POKÉBALLS	200 POKÉBALLS
🪙 100	🪙 460	🪙 800

INCENSE	8 INCENSE	25 INCENSE
🪙 80	🪙 500	🪙 1250

1
Collect now!

Spend your winnings on all sorts of essential Poké-kit.

WHAT'S IN STORE

There are loads of items available in the store that you can spend your PokéCoins on. While you can buy PokéCoins with real cash, it is a much better idea to win them through holding Gyms. After a while you'll have a regular supply of PokéCoins to keep topping up your supply of PokéBalls, Lures, Lucky Eggs, and Incubators to keep you on track to becoming a Pokémon master. Here is the complete list of what is available in store.

PokéBalls

20 PokéBalls	100 PokeCoins
100 PokéBalls	460 PokeCoins
200 PokéBalls	800 PokeCoins

Incense

1 Incense	80 PokeCoins
8 Incense	500 PokeCoins
25 Incense	1250 PokeCoins

Lucky Eggs

1 Lucky Egg	80 PokeCoins
8 Lucky Eggs	500 PokeCoins
25 Lucky Eggs	1250 PokeCoins

Lure Modules

1 Lure Module	100 PokeCoins
8 Lure Modules	680 PokeCoins

Other Items

Incubator	150 PokeCoins
Bag Upgrade	200 PokeCoins
Pokémon Storage Upgrade	200 PokeCoins

LUCKY EGG   8 LUCKY EGGS   25 LUCKY EGGS

80   500   1250

LURE MODULE   8 LURE MODULES   EGG INCUBATOR

100   680   150

UPGRADES

BAG UPGRADE   POKÉMON STORAGE UPGRADE

Spend your PokéCoins wisely...

STORAGE

One of the most important items you can buy is more storage for your items and Pokémon. Each upgrade costs 200 PokéCoins and will increase the number of items or Pokémon you can carry by 50. The maximum you can increase your storage capacity to is 1000 for both your items and Pokémon storage facilities. Once this maximum level has been reached, you will be unable to purchase any more upgrades.

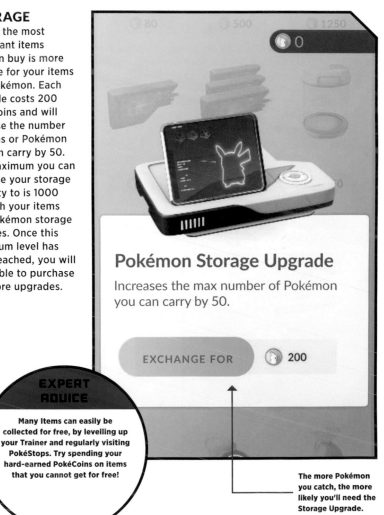

Pokémon Storage Upgrade

Increases the max number of Pokémon you can carry by 50.

EXCHANGE FOR   200

EXPERT ADVICE

Many items can easily be collected for free, by levelling up your Trainer and regularly visiting PokéStops. Try spending your hard-earned PokéCoins on items that you cannot get for free!

The more Pokémon you catch, the more likely you'll need the Storage Upgrade.

WHAT'S NEXT?

GENERATION 2 IS COMING

Almost immediately after Pokémon Go was released, players were already looking forward to the second generation. While it seemed almost inevitable that it would happen at some point, for a long while much of the speculation was purely guesswork, and had little fact to back it up. However, at San Diego Comic Con 2016, Niantic founder John Hanke confirmed that Pokémon Go's Second Generation is coming sometime in 2017. Let's take a look at what players can expect...

LEGENDARY BIRDS

There have been so many rumours about the three legendary birds and how they might become available in Pokémon Go. The truth is, we still don't really know how Moltres, Articuno, and Zapdos will be obtainable, but we do know that they are coming!

THE MISSING POKÉMON

We also believe that the other missing Pokémon from the first generation will be available in Pokémon Go's second generation. This means we should expect to see Mew, Mewtwo, and Ditto as well. Again we do not know how, but their inclusion is highly likely.

We'll soon see the legendary birds, one of whom is shown here as a team emblem.

There are spaces on the Pokédex for Mew, Mewtwo, and Ditto.

THE SECOND GENERATION

The second generation of Pokémon come from the Johto region of the Pokémon world, and were originally released in Pokémon Gold, Silver, and Crystal. In this series, another 100 Pokémon were added to the total number of Pokémon available. This included baby evolutions, and new evolved forms of some of the existing first generation Pokémon.

Get ready to create your own Eggs.

4.01 / 5 km

Walk to hatch this Egg.

Save your Candies to evolve your Pokémon, like this Zubat into a Crobat.

BABY POKÉMON

The second generation introduced baby Pokémon to the game, and it's rumoured that all of the following baby Pokémon will be available. The most exciting thing about this is the likely introduction of a breeding system so you can create your own Eggs.

PICHU
CLEFFA
IGGLYBUFF
TYROGUE
MAGBY
ELEKID

LEGACY EVOLUTIONS

The second generation contains a number of Pokémon that evolve from Pokémon available in the first generation. This means you can start saving Candies now and get yourself ready for these amazing Pokémon. The following Pokémon all fit into this category.

CROBAT
STEELIX
POLITOED
SLOWKING
BELLOSSUM
SCIZOR
UMBREON
ESPEON
PORYGON2

THE COMPLETE LIST

The second generation of Pokémon games introduced some amazing new Pokémon to the game. Here is the complete list of Pokémon that first appeared in Pokémon Gold, Silver, and Crystal:

No.	Name	Type	No.	Name	Type
152	CHIKORITA	Grass	202	WOBBUFFET	Psychic
153	BAYLEEF	Grass	203	GIRAFARIG	Normal/Psychic
154	MEGANIUM	Grass	204	PINECO	Bug
155	CYNDAQUIL	Fire	205	FORRETRESS	Bug/Steel
156	QUILAVA	Fire	206	DUNSPARCE	Normal
157	TYPHLOSION	Fire	207	GLIGAR	Ground/Flying
158	TOTODILE	Water	208	STEELIX	Steel/Ground
159	CROCONAW	Water	209	SNUBBULL	Normal
160	FERALIGATR	Water	210	GRANBULL	Normal
161	SENTRET	Normal	211	QWILFISH	Water/Poison
162	FURRET	Normal	212	SCIZOR	Bug/Steel
163	HOOTHOOT	Normal/Flying	213	SHUCKLE	Bug/Rock
164	NOCTOWL	Normal/Flying	214	HERACROSS	Bug/Fighting
165	LEDYBA	Bug/Flying	215	SNEASEL	Dark/Ice
166	LEDIAN	Bug/Flying	216	TEDDIURSA	Normal
167	SPINARAK	Bug/Poison	217	URSARING	Normal
168	ARIADOS	Bug/Poison	218	SLUGMA	Fire
169	CROBAT	Poison/Flying	219	MAGCARGO	Fire/Rock
170	CHINCHOU	Water/Electric	220	SWINUB	Ice/Ground
171	LANTURN	Water/Electric	221	PILOSWINE	Ice/Ground
172	PICHU	Electric	222	CORSOLA	Water/Rock
173	CLEFFA	Normal	223	REMORAID	Water
174	IGGLYBUFF	Normal	224	OCTILLERY	Water
175	TOGEPI	Normal	225	DELIBIRD	Ice/Flying
176	TOGETIC	Normal/Flying	226	MANTINE	Water/Flying
177	NATU	Psychic/Flying	227	SKARMORY	Steel/Flying
178	XATU	Psychic/Flying	228	HOUNDOUR	Dark/Fire
179	MAREEP	Electric	229	HOUNDOOM	Dark/Fire
180	FLAAFFY	Electric	230	KINGDRA	Water/Dragon
181	AMPHAROS	Electric	231	PHANPY	Ground
182	BELLOSSOM	Grass	232	DONPHAN	Ground
183	MARILL	Water	233	PORYGON2	Normal
184	AZUMARILL	Water	234	STANTLER	Normal
185	SUDOWOODO	Rock	235	SMEARGLE	Normal
186	POLITOED	Water	236	TYROGUE	Fighting
187	HOPPIP	Grass/Flying	237	HITMONTOP	Fighting
188	SKIPLOOM	Grass/Flying	238	SMOOCHUM	Ice/Psychic
189	JUMPLUFF	Grass/Flying	239	ELEKID	Electric
190	AIPOM	Normal	240	MAGBY	Fire
191	SUNKERN	Grass	241	MILTANK	Normal
192	SUNFLORA	Grass	242	BLISSEY	Normal
193	YANMA	Bug/Flying	243	RAIKOU	Electric
194	WOOPER	Water/Ground	244	ENTEI	Fire
195	QUAGSIRE	Water/Ground	245	SUICUNE	Water
196	ESPEON	Psychic	246	LARVITAR	Rock/Ground
197	UMBREON	Dark	247	PUPITAR	Rock/Ground
198	MURKROW	Dark/Flying	248	TYRANITAR	Rock/Dark
199	SLOWKING	Water/Psychic	249	LUGIA	Psychic/Flying
200	MISDREAVUS	Ghost	250	HO-OH	Fire/Flying
201	UNOWN	Psychic			

It might be a while before these appear...

THE LEGENDARIES

Niantic have hinted that the second generation will increase the number of available Pokémon by 100. With the first generation legendaries not being available until this release, it would therefore make perfect sense that the second generation legendaries will not be included (not at launch, at least).

In that case, we doubt these Pokémon will be included!

LUGIA
HO-OH
CELEBI
RAIKOU
SUICUNE
ENTEI

NEW MOVES

Niantic have suggested that, along with the amazing list of new Pokémon available in the second generation, we are also going to be treated to no fewer than 86 new moves. Although the list has not been released at this time, this is really good news, and these moves may even be available for existing first generation Pokémon, which is very exciting.

You'll soon be able to add new moves to your first generation Pokémon.

REGION-SPECIFIC POKÉMON

We are led to believe that four of the second generation Pokémon available have been singled out to be region-specific Pokémon, just like Tauros, Mr. Mime, Farfetch'd and Kangaskhan. Our best guess would be that these Pokémon will be ones that have no evolution tree. Smeargle, Heracross, Delibird, Sudowoodo, Dunsparce, or Stantler could be possibilities.

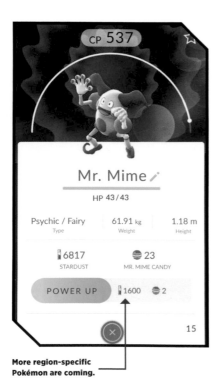

CP 537

Mr. Mime

HP 43/43

Psychic / Fairy	61.91 kg	1.18 m
Type	Weight	Height

6817
STARDUST

23
MR. MIME CANDY

POWER UP   1600   2

15

More region-specific Pokémon are coming.

PVP BATTLES

While battling Gyms is fun, players have been calling for a player vs player battle mode since the game was first released. Being able to take on your friend's best Pokémon and earn some bragging rights is a perfect way to practice for your Gym battles. We are really looking forward to this new feature!

TRADING

There have been plenty of rumours that the next generation will feature a trade system. This is something that has always been integral to the Pokémon franchise, and we're sure this will be added at some point. It's possible that this feature might only be possible when two gaming devices are nearby.

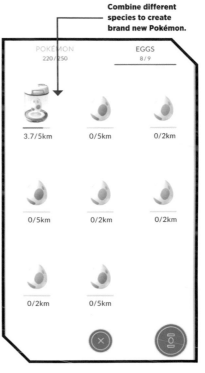

Combine different species to create brand new Pokémon.

Trade your way to a complete collection.

BREEDING

As baby Pokémon are included in Generation 2, it is very likely that a new breeding mechanism may be added to the game. This may also be why Ditto has not been released yet. This is really exciting news, as great rewards can be gained by devoting time and effort into breeding the right Pokémon.

POKÉMON GO EXPERT BATTLE GUIDE

POKÉ PROFILES

WHAT HAVE I CAUGHT?

This section lists the First Generation Pokémon in order, with their best quick moves, their best power (or charge) moves, their strongest and weakest opponents, and the Pokémon's type in an easy-to-find way.

Use the key below to quickly check what type of Pokémon you've caught, and what that means for your Battle prospects...

KEY

○ NORMAL

● WATER

● DRAGON

● POISON

● ELECTRIC

● FIRE

● FIGHTING

● GROUND

● ICE

● GRASS

● FLYING

● ROCK

● FAIRY

● PSYCHIC

● GHOST

● BUG

● STEEL

001 BULBASAUR

CP 109

Bulbasaur ✎

HP 28/28

Grass / Poison
Type

12.44 kg
Weight

0.93 m
Height

🗲110
STARDUST

● 19
BULBASAUR CANDY

BEST QUICK MOVE
Vine Whip

STRONG AGAINST
● ●

BEST POWER MOVE
Power Whip

WEAK AGAINST
● ● ● ●

002 IVYSAUR

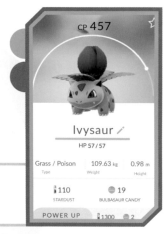

CP 457

Ivysaur ✎

HP 57/57

Grass / Poison
Type

109.63 kg
Weight

0.98 m
Height

🗲110
STARDUST

● 19
BULBASAUR CANDY

POWER UP   🗲1300 ● 2

BEST QUICK MOVE
Vine Whip

STRONG AGAINST
● ●

BEST POWER MOVE
Solar Beam

WEAK AGAINST
● ● ● ●

003 VENUSAUR

CP 32

Venusaur ✎

HP 16/16

Grass / Poison
Type

123.69 kg
Weight

2.1 m
Height

🗲14402
STARDUST

● 18
BULBASAUR CANDY

BEST QUICK MOVE
Vine Whip

STRONG AGAINST
● ●

BEST POWER MOVE
Solar Beam

WEAK AGAINST
● ● ● ●

004 CHARMANDER

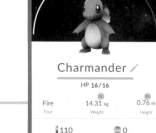

CP 52

Charmander ✎

HP 16/16

Fire
Type

14.31 kg
Weight

0.76 m
Height

🗲110
STARDUST

● 0
CHARMANDER CANDY

POWER UP   🗲200 ● 1

BEST QUICK MOVE
Scratch

STRONG AGAINST
● ● ● ●

BEST POWER MOVE
Flamethrower

WEAK AGAINST
● ● ●

KEY	○ Normal	● Grass	● Dragon	● Rock
	● Water	● Flying	● Poison	● Fairy

005 CHARMELEON

CP 200

BEST QUICK MOVE
Scratch

STRONG AGAINST
● ● ● ●

BEST POWER MOVE
Flamethrower

WEAK AGAINST
● ● ●

Charmeleon ✏

HP 38 / 38

Fire	25.44 kg	1.26 m
Type	Weight	Height

🔥4900
UST

🍬3
CHARMANDER CANDY

CP 883

006 CHARIZARD

BEST QUICK MOVE
Wing Attack

STRONG AGAINST
● ● ● ●

BEST POWER MOVE
Fire Blast

WEAK AGAINST
● ●

Charizard ✏

HP 80 / 80

Fire / Flying	125.8 kg	2.02 m
Type	Weight	Height

🔥3261
STARDUST

🍬25
CHARMANDER CANDY

007 SQUIRTLE

CP 282

BEST QUICK MOVE
Bubble

STRONG AGAINST
● ● ●

BEST POWER MOVE
Aqua Tail

WEAK AGAINST
● ●

Squirtle ✏

HP 42 / 42

Water	9.65 kg	0.52 m
Type	Weight	Height

🔥110
STARDUST

🍬8
SQUIRTLE CANDY

CP 353

Wartortle ✏

HP 51 / 51

Water	6.84 kg	0.96 m
Type	Weight	Height

🔥43813
STARDUST

🍬2
SQUIRTLE CANDY

008 WARTORTLE

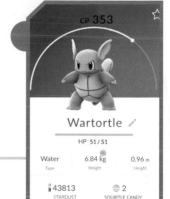

BEST QUICK MOVE
Water Gun

STRONG AGAINST
● ● ●

BEST POWER MOVE
Hydro Pump

WEAK AGAINST
● ●

○ Electric	● Psychic	● Fighting	● Bug	● Ice
● Fire	● Ghost	● Ground	○ Steel	

009 BLASTOISE

CP 322

Blastoise

HP 48 / 48

Water	86.77 kg	1.52 m
Type	Weight	Height

1230	3
STARDUST	SQUIRTLE CANDY

600   1

BEST QUICK MOVE
Water Gun

BEST POWER MOVE
Hydro Pump

STRONG AGAINST

WEAK AGAINST

010 CATERPIE

BEST QUICK MOVE
Bug Bite

BEST POWER MOVE
Struggle

STRONG AGAINST

WEAK AGAINST

CP 53

Caterpie

HP 30 / 30

Bug	4.16 kg	0.35 m
Type	Weight	Height

110	21
STARDUST	CATERPIE CANDY

POWER UP   600   1

011 METAPOD

CP 77

Metapod

HP 41 / 41

Bug	1.26 kg	0.76 m
Type	Weight	Height

43813	1
STARDUST	CATERPIE CANDY

POWER UP   800   1

BEST QUICK MOVE
Bug Bite

BEST POWER MOVE
Struggle

STRONG AGAINST

WEAK AGAINST

012 BUTTERFREE

BEST QUICK MOVE
Bug Bite

BEST POWER MOVE
Bug Buzz

STRONG AGAINST

WEAK AGAINST

CP 233

Butterfree

HP   43 / 43

Bug / Flying	32 kg	1.18 m
Type	Weight	Height

110	21
STARDUST	CATERPIE CANDY

KEY			
○ Normal	Grass	Dragon	Rock
Water	Flying	Poison	Fairy

013 WEEDLE

CP 25

Weedle ✎

HP 20/20

Bug / Poison — Type
1.89 kg — Weight
0.25 m — Height

800 — STARDUST
3 — WEEDLE CANDY

400 1

BEST QUICK MOVE
Bug Bite

BEST POWER MOVE
Struggle

STRONG AGAINST
● ●

WEAK AGAINST
● ● ● ●

014 KAKUNA

CP 197

Kakuna ✎

HP 51/51

Bug / Poison — Type
3.74 kg — Weight
0.65 m — Height

43813 — STARDUST
17 — WEEDLE CANDY

2200 2

BEST QUICK MOVE
Bug Bite

BEST POWER MOVE
Struggle

STRONG AGAINST
● ●

WEAK AGAINST
● ● ● ●

015 BEEDRILL

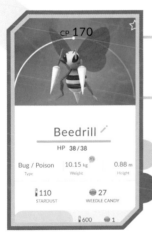

CP 170

Beedrill ✎

HP 38/38

Bug / Poison — Type
10.15 kg — Weight
0.88 m — Height

110 — STARDUST
27 — WEEDLE CANDY

600 1

BEST QUICK MOVE
Poison Jab

BEST POWER MOVE
Sludge Bomb

STRONG AGAINST
● ●

WEAK AGAINST
● ● ● ●

016 PIDGEY

CP 192

Pidgey ✎

HP 40/40

Normal / Flying — Type
2.84 kg — Weight
0.37 m — Height

1476 — STARDUST
87 — PIDGEY CANDY

BEST QUICK MOVE
Tackle

BEST POWER MOVE
Aerial Ace

STRONG AGAINST
● ● ●

WEAK AGAINST
● ●

| Electric | ● Psychic | ● Fighting | ● Bug | ● Ice |
| ● Fire | ● Ghost | ● Ground | Steel | |

CP 255

Pidgeotto ✎

HP 21 / 54

Normal / Flying	2.89 kg	0.95 m
Type	Weight	Height

🔹2347
STARDUST

🍬50
PIDGEY CANDY

017 PIDGEOTTO

BEST QUICK MOVE
Wing Attack

BEST POWER MOVE
Aerial Ace

STRONG AGAINST
● ● ●

WEAK AGAINST
● ● ●

CP 567

Pidgeot ✎

HP 75 / 75

Normal / Flying	21.82 kg	1.43 m
Type	Weight	Height

🔹110
STARDUST

🍬37
PIDGEY CANDY

POWER UP 🔹1000 🍬1

018 PIDGEOT

BEST QUICK MOVE
Wing Attack

BEST POWER MOVE
Hurricane

STRONG AGAINST
● ● ●

WEAK AGAINST
● ● ●

CP 195

Rattata ✎

HP 34 / 34

Normal	4.4 kg	0.33 m
Type	Weight	Height

🔹110
STARDUST

🍬46
RATTATA CANDY

POWER UP 🔹1600 🍬2

019 RATTATA

BEST QUICK MOVE
Tackle

BEST POWER MOVE
Body Slam

STRONG AGAINST

WEAK AGAINST
●

CP 141

Raticate ✎

HP 31 / 31

Normal	1.88 kg	0.77 m
Type	Weight	Height

🔹110
STARDUST

🍬46
RATTATA CANDY

POWER UP 🔹400 🍬1

020 RATICATE

BEST QUICK MOVE
Bite

BEST POWER MOVE
Hyper Beam

STRONG AGAINST

WEAK AGAINST
●

KEY	○ Normal	● Grass	● Dragon	● Rock
	● Water	● Flying	● Poison	● Fairy

021 SPEAROW

BEST QUICK MOVE
Peck

BEST POWER MOVE
Drill Peck

STRONG AGAINST
● ● ●

WEAK AGAINST
● ●

CP 235

Spearow ✏

HP 45/45

Normal / Flying	2.81 kg	0.36 m
Type	Weight	Height

▮110
STARDUST

🍬37
SPEAROW CANDY

---

022 FEAROW

CP 470

Fearow ✏

HP 59/59

Normal / Flying	8.23 kg	1.28 m
Type	Weight	Height

▮110
STARDUST

🍬37
SPEAROW CANDY

POWER UP ▮1000 🍬1

BEST QUICK MOVE
Steel Wing

BEST POWER MOVE
Drill Wing

STRONG AGAINST
● ● ●

WEAK AGAINST
● ●

---

023 EKANS

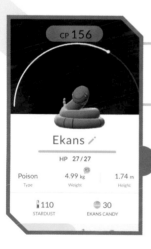

CP 156

BEST QUICK MOVE
Poison Sting

BEST POWER MOVE
Gunk Shot

STRONG AGAINST
● ●

WEAK AGAINST
● ●

Ekans ✏

HP 27/27

Poison	4.99 kg	1.74 m
Type	Weight	Height

▮110
STARDUST

🍬30
EKANS CANDY

---

024 ARBOK

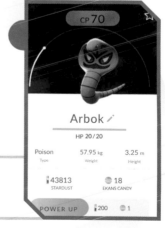

CP 70

Arbok ✏

HP 20/20

Poison	57.95 kg	3.25 m
Type	Weight	Height

▮43813
STARDUST

🍬18
EKANS CANDY

POWER UP ▮200 🍬1

BEST QUICK MOVE
Bite

BEST POWER MOVE
Gunk Shot

STRONG AGAINST
● ●

WEAK AGAINST
● ●

● Electric	● Psychic	● Fighting	● Bug	● Ice
● Fire	● Ghost	● Ground	● Steel	

025 PIKACHU

CP 11

BEST QUICK MOVE
Thunder Shock

BEST POWER MOVE
Thunder

STRONG AGAINST

WEAK AGAINST

Pikachu

HP 10 / 10

Electric	10.1 kg	0.5 m
Type	Weight	Height

100 STARDUST 3 PIKACHU CANDY

POWER UP 200 1

026 RAICHU

CP 249

Raichu

HP 35 / 35

Electric	37.76 kg	0.87 m
Type	Weight	Height

2700 STARDUST 1 PIKACHU CANDY

POWER UP 600 1

BEST QUICK MOVE
Spark

BEST POWER MOVE
Thunder

STRONG AGAINST

WEAK AGAINST

027 SANDSHREW

CP 107

BEST QUICK MOVE
Mud Shot

BEST POWER MOVE
Dig

STRONG AGAINST

WEAK AGAINST

Sandshrew

HP 33 / 33

Ground	10.38 kg	0.58 m
Type	Weight	Height

110 STARDUST 7 SANDSHREW CANDY

POWER UP 600 1

028 SANDSLASH

CP 626

Sandslash

HP 75 / 75

Ground	23.71 kg	0.58 m
Type	Weight	Height

7507 STARDUST 3 SANDSHREW CANDY

POWER UP 1600 2

BEST QUICK MOVE
Mud Shot

BEST POWER MOVE
Earthquake

STRONG AGAINST

WEAK AGAINST

KEY

○ Normal	Grass	Dragon	Rock
Water	Flying	Poison	Fairy

029 NIDORAN ♀

CP 257

Nidoran ♀ ✎

HP 57 / 57

Poison	6.89 kg	0.43 m
Type	Weight	Height

🔹110
STARDUST

🍬15
NIDORAN CANDY

POWER UP　　🔹1300　🍬2

BEST QUICK MOVE
Poison Sting

BEST POWER MOVE
Sludge Bomb

STRONG AGAINST
●　●

WEAK AGAINST
●　●

030 NIDORINA

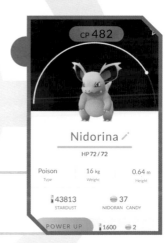

CP 482

Nidorina ✎

HP 72 / 72

Poison	16 kg	0.64 m
Type	Weight	Height

🔹43813
STARDUST

🍬37
NIDORAN CANDY

POWER UP　　🔹1600　🍬2

BEST QUICK MOVE
Poison Sting

BEST POWER MOVE
Sludge Bomb

STRONG AGAINST
●　●

WEAK AGAINST
●　●

031 NIDOQUEEN

CP 394

Nidoqueen ✎

HP 60 / 60

Poison / Ground	45.04 kg	1.05 m
Type	Weight	Height

🔹900

🍬7
NIDORAN CANDY

🔹600　🍬1

BEST QUICK MOVE
Poison Jab

BEST POWER MOVE
Earthquake

STRONG AGAINST
●　○　●

WEAK AGAINST
●　●　●　●

032 NIDORAN ♂

CP 79

Nidoran ♂ ✎

HP 27 / 27

Poison	6.83 kg	0.44 m
Type	Weight	Height

🔹110
STARDUST

🍬15
NIDORAN CANDY

POWER UP　　🔹400　🍬1

BEST QUICK MOVE
Poison Sting

BEST POWER MOVE
Body Slam

STRONG AGAINST
●　●

WEAK AGAINST
●　●

○ Electric	● Psychic	● Fighting	○ Bug	○ Ice
● Fire	● Ghost	● Ground	○ Steel	

033 NIDORINO

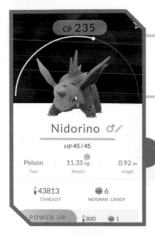

CP 235

Nidorino ♂ ✎

HP 45 / 45

Poison	11.35 kg	0.92 m
Type	Weight	Height

43813 STARDUST — 6 NIDORAN CANDY

POWER UP 800 1

BEST QUICK MOVE
Poison Jab

BEST POWER MOVE
Sludge Bomb

STRONG AGAINST
● ●

WEAK AGAINST
● ●

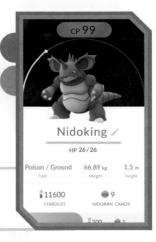

CP 99

Nidoking ✎

HP 26 / 26

Poison / Ground	66.89 kg	1.5 m
Type	Weight	Height

11600 STARDUST — 9 NIDORAN CANDY

200 1

034 NIDOKING

BEST QUICK MOVE
Poison Jab

BEST POWER MOVE
Earthquake

STRONG AGAINST
● ○ ●

WEAK AGAINST
● ● ● ●

035 CLEFAIRY

CP 81

Clefairy ✎

HP 32 / 32

Fairy	8.27 kg	0.63 m
Type	Weight	Height

300 STARDUST — 3 CLEFAIRY CANDY

POWER UP 400 1

BEST QUICK MOVE
Pound

BEST POWER MOVE
Moonblast

STRONG AGAINST
● ●

WEAK AGAINST
● ○

CP 164

Clefable ✎

HP 42 / 42

Fairy	50.73 kg	1.59m
Type	Weight	Height

1300 STARDUST — 6 CLEFAIRY CANDY

POWER UP 400 1

036 CLEFABLE

BEST QUICK MOVE
Pound

BEST POWER MOVE
Moonblast

STRONG AGAINST
● ● ●

WEAK AGAINST
● ○

KEY	○ Normal	● Grass	● Dragon	● Rock
	● Water	○ Flying	● Poison	● Fairy

037 VULPIX

CP 10

Vulpix ✎

HP 10/10

Fire	12.36 kg	0.69 m
Type	Weight	Height

⬛ 2341 STARDUST ⬤ 3 VULPIX CANDY

POWER UP ⬛ 200 ⬤ 1

BEST QUICK MOVE
Ember

BEST POWER MOVE
Flamethrower

STRONG AGAINST
⬤ ⬤ ⬤ ⬤

WEAK AGAINST
⬤ ⬤ ⬤

038 NINETALES

BEST QUICK MOVE
Ember

BEST POWER MOVE
Fire Blast

STRONG AGAINST
⬤ ⬤ ⬤ ⬤

WEAK AGAINST
⬤ ⬤ ⬤

CP 398

Ninetales ✎

HP 54/54

Fire	21.92 kg	1.08 m
Type	Weight	Height

⬛ 552 STARDUST ⬤ 4 VULPIX CANDY

POWER UP ⬛ 800 ⬤ 1

039 JIGGLYPUFF

CP 233

Jigglypuff ✎

HP 98/98

Normal / Fairy	4.8 kg	0.5 m
Type	Weight	Height

⬛ 110 STARDUST ⬤ 15 JIGGLYPUFF CANDY

POWER UP ⬛ 1000 ⬤ 1

BEST QUICK MOVE
Pound

BEST POWER MOVE
Bodyslam

STRONG AGAINST
⬤ ⬤

WEAK AGAINST
⬤ ⬤

040 WIGGLYTUFF

BEST QUICK MOVE
Pound

BEST POWER MOVE
Hyper Beam

STRONG AGAINST
⬤ ⬤

WEAK AGAINST
⬤ ⬤

CP 28

Wigglytuff ✎

HP 27/27

Normal / Fairy	12.37 kg	0.97 m
Type	Weight	Height

⬛ 3600 STARDUST ⬤ 9 JIGGLYPUFF CANDY

⬤ Electric	⬤ Psychic	⬤ Fighting	⬤ Bug	⬤ Ice
⬤ Fire	⬤ Ghost	⬤ Ground	⬤ Steel	

041 ZUBAT

CP 184

Zubat

HP 38/38

Poison / Flying	8.79 kg	0.81 m
Type	Weight	Height

🔹110
STARDUST

🔴42
ZUBAT CANDY

POWER UP · 1300 · 2

BEST QUICK MOVE
Bite

BEST POWER MOVE
Sludge Bomb

STRONG AGAINST
● ● ● ●

WEAK AGAINST
● ● ● ○

042 GOLBAT

CP 479

Golbat

HP 76/76

Poison / Flying	71.62 kg	1.67 m
Type	Weight	Height

🔹110
STARDUST

🔴42
ZUBAT CANDY

POWER UP · 1600 · 2

BEST QUICK MOVE
Wing Attack

BEST POWER MOVE
Air Cutter

STRONG AGAINST
● ● ● ●

WEAK AGAINST
● ● ● ○

043 ODDISH

CP 368

Oddish

HP 47/47

Grass / Poison	4.65 kg	0.41 m
Type	Weight	Height

🔹110
STARDUST

🔴18
ODDISH CANDY

· 1600 · 2

BEST QUICK MOVE
Razor Leaf

BEST POWER MOVE
Sludge Bomb

STRONG AGAINST
● ●

WEAK AGAINST
● ● ○ ●

044 GLOOM

CP 271

Gloom

HP 43/43

Grass / Poison	4.09 kg	0.71 m
Type	Weight	Height

🔹43813
STARDUST

🔴5
ODDISH CANDY

· 600 · 1

BEST QUICK MOVE
Razor Leaf

BEST POWER MOVE
Sludge Bomb

STRONG AGAINST
● ●

WEAK AGAINST
● ● ● ●

KEY

○ Normal	● Grass	● Dragon	● Rock
● Water	● Flying	● Poison	● Fairy

045 VILEPLUME

CP 516

Vileplume ✏

HP 58 / 58

Grass / Poison	15.04 kg	1.18 m
Type	Weight	Height

🔹606
STARDUST

🍬37
ODDISH CANDY

🔹800

BEST QUICK MOVE
Razor Leaf

BEST POWER MOVE
Solar Beam

STRONG AGAINST
● ●

WEAK AGAINST
● ● ● ●

046 PARAS

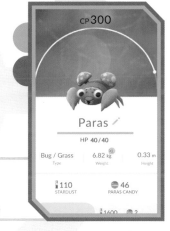

CP 300

Paras ✏

HP 40 / 40

Bug / Grass	6.82 kg	0.33 m
Type	Weight	Height

🔹110
STARDUST

🍬46
PARAS CANDY

🔹1600

BEST QUICK MOVE
Bug Bite

BEST POWER MOVE
Seed Bomb

STRONG AGAINST
● ● ● ●

WEAK AGAINST
● ● ● ● ● ●

047 PARASECT

CP 521

Parasect ✏

HP 57 / 57

Bug / Grass	24.6 kg	1.05 m
Type	Weight	Height

🔹110
STARDUST

🍬46
PARAS CANDY

BEST QUICK MOVE
Bug Bite

BEST POWER MOVE
Solar Beam

STRONG AGAINST
● ● ● ●

WEAK AGAINST
● ● ● ● ● ●

048 VENONAT

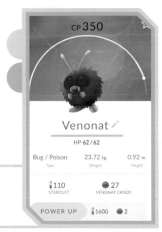

CP 350

Venonat ✏

HP 62 / 62

Bug / Poison	23.72 kg	0.92 m
Type	Weight	Height

🔹110
STARDUST

🍬27
VENONAT CANDY

POWER UP   🔹1600 🍬2

BEST QUICK MOVE
Bug Bite

BEST POWER MOVE
Signal Beam

STRONG AGAINST
● ●

WEAK AGAINST
● ● ● ●

○ Electric	● Psychic	● Fighting	● Bug	● Ice
● Fire	● Ghost	● Ground	● Steel	

049 VENOMOTH

CP 666

Venomoth ✎

HP 70 / 70

Bug / Poison	16.53 kg	1.13 m
Type	Weight	Height

🔷 1256
STARDUST

🔵 1
VENONAT CANDY

POWER UP   🔷 1600   🔵 2

BEST QUICK MOVE
Bug Bite

BEST POWER MOVE
Bug Buzz

STRONG AGAINST

WEAK AGAINST

050 DIGLETT

BEST QUICK MOVE
Mud Slap

BEST POWER MOVE
Dig

STRONG AGAINST

WEAK AGAINST

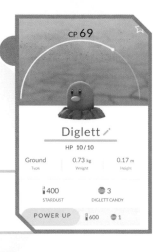

CP 69

Diglett ✎

HP 10 / 10

Ground	0.73 kg	0.17 m
Type	Weight	Height

🔷 400
STARDUST

🔵 3
DIGLETT CANDY

POWER UP   🔷 600   🔵 1

051 DUGTRIO

BEST QUICK MOVE
Mud Slap

BEST POWER MOVE
Stone Age

STRONG AGAINST

WEAK AGAINST

CP 411

Dugtrio ✎

HP 37 / 37

Ground	33.3 kg	0.81 m
Type	Weight	Height

🔷 28227
STARDUST

🔵 7
DIGLETT CANDY

POWER UP   🔷 1600   🔵 2

052 MEOWTH

BEST QUICK MOVE
Scratch

BEST POWER MOVE
Body Slam

STRONG AGAINST

WEAK AGAINST

CP 253

Meowth ✎

HP 44 / 44

Normal	4.91 kg	0.44 m
Type	Weight	Height

🔷 43813
STARDUST

🔵 14
MEOWTH CANDY

POWER UP   🔷 1600   🔵 2

KEY

◯ Normal	🟢 Grass	🟣 Dragon	🔴 Rock
🔵 Water	🟡 Flying	🟣 Poison	🔴 Fairy

053 PERSIAN

CP 760

Persian ✎

HP 77 / 77

Normal Type	32 kg Weight	0.97 m Height

⚡87419 STARDUST	⚫ 17 MEOWTH CANDY

POWER UP ⚡2200 ⚫ 2

BEST QUICK MOVE
Scratch

STRONG AGAINST

BEST POWER MOVE
Play Rough

WEAK AGAINST
⚫

054 PSYDUCK

CP 94

Psyduck ✎

HP 26 / 26

Water Type	7.7 kg Weight	0.62 m Height

⚡110 STARDUST	⚫ 3 PSYDUCK CANDY

POWER UP ⚡400 ⚫ 1

BEST QUICK MOVE
Water Gun

STRONG AGAINST
⚫ ⚫ ⚫

BEST POWER MOVE
Hydro Pump

WEAK AGAINST
⚫

055 GOLDUCK

CP 479

Golduck ✎

HP 60 / 60

Water Type	46.35 kg Weight	1.34 m Height

⚡463 STARDUST	⚫ 0 PSYDUCK CANDY

POWER UP ⚡800 ⚫ 1

BEST QUICK MOVE
Water Gun

STRONG AGAINST
⚫ ⚫ ⚫

BEST POWER MOVE
Hydro Pump

WEAK AGAINST
⚫ ⚫

056 MANKEY

CP 255

Mankey ✎

HP 40 / 40

Fighting Type	24.52 kg Weight	0.45 m Height

⚡43813 STARDUST	⚫ 21 MANKEY CANDY

POWER UP ⚡1300 ⚫ 2

BEST QUICK MOVE
Scratch

STRONG AGAINST
○ ⚫ ⚫ ⚫

BEST POWER MOVE
Cross Chop

WEAK AGAINST
⚫ ⚫ ⚫

○ Electric	⚫ Psychic	⚫ Fighting	⚫ Bug	⚫ Ice
⚫ Fire	⚫ Ghost	⚫ Ground	○ Steel	

057 PRIMEAPE

Primeape ✎

HP 55 / 55

Fighting	20.68 kg	0.91 m
Type	Weight	Height

📊 400
STARDUST

🍬 1
MANKEY CANDY

💊 1000

BEST QUICK MOVE
Low Kick

BEST POWER MOVE
Cross Chop

STRONG AGAINST
○ ● ● ●

WEAK AGAINST
● ● ●

058 GROWLITHE

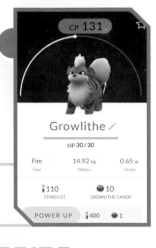

Growlithe ✎

HP 30 / 30

Fire	14.92 kg	0.65 m
Type	Weight	Height

📊 110
STARDUST

🍬 10
GROWLITHE CANDY

POWER UP   📊 400   🍬 1

BEST QUICK MOVE
Bite

BEST POWER MOVE
Flamethrower

STRONG AGAINST
● ● ● ●

WEAK AGAINST
● ● ●

059 ARCANINE

Arcanine ✎

HP 101 / 101

Fire	155 kg	1.98 m
Type	Weight	Height

📊 43867
STARDUST

🍬 26
GROWLITHE CANDY

POWER UP   📊 1900   🍬 2

BEST QUICK MOVE
Fire Fang

BEST POWER MOVE
Fire Blast

STRONG AGAINST
● ● ● ●

WEAK AGAINST
● ● ●

060 POLIWAG

Poliwag ✎

HP 17 / 17

Water	11.18 kg	0.35 m
Type	Weight	Height

📊 12600
STARDUST

🍬 9
POLIWAG CANDY

POWER UP   📊 400   🍬 1

BEST QUICK MOVE
Bubble

BEST POWER MOVE
Body Slam

STRONG AGAINST
● ● ● ● ●

WEAK AGAINST
● ● ● ●

POKÉMON GO EXPERT BATTLE GUIDE

KEY

○ Normal	● Grass	● Dragon	● Rock
● Water	● Flying	● Poison	● Fairy

061 POLIWHIRL

CP 172

Poliwhirl ✎

HP 41 / 41

Water	15.56 kg	1.06 m
Type	Weight	Height

🔸43813   🟤79
STARDUST   POLIWAG CANDY

POWER UP   🔸600   🟤1

BEST QUICK MOVE
Bubble

BEST POWER MOVE
Scald

STRONG AGAINST
● ● ● ● ●

WEAK AGAINST
● ● ● ●

062 POLIWRATH

BEST QUICK MOVE
Bubble

BEST POWER MOVE
Hydro Pump

STRONG AGAINST
○ ● ● ● ● ●

WEAK AGAINST
● ● ● ●

CP 688

Poliwrath ✎

HP 79 / 79

Water / Fighting	52.63 kg	1.29 m
Type	Weight	Height

🔸110   🟤19
STARDUST   POLIWAG CANDY

🔸1000   🟤1

063 ABRA

CP 103

Abra ✎

HP 18 / 18

Psychic	10.17 kg	0.77 m
Type	Weight	Height

🔸110   🟤7
STARDUST   ABRA CANDY

POWER UP   🔸800   🟤1

BEST QUICK MOVE
Zen Headbutt

BEST POWER MOVE
Psyshock

STRONG AGAINST
● ●

WEAK AGAINST
● ●

064 KADABRA

BEST QUICK MOVE
Psycho Cut

BEST POWER MOVE
Shadow Ball

STRONG AGAINST
● ●

WEAK AGAINST
● ●

CP 353

Kadabra ✎

HP 40 / 40

Psychic	57.31 kg	1.23 m
Type	Weight	Height

🔸1457   🟤27
STARDUST   ABRA CANDY

POWER UP   🔸1300   🟤2

○ Electric   ● Psychic   ● Fighting   ● Bug   ● Ice
● Fire   ● Ghost   ● Ground   ● Steel

065 ALAKAZAM

CP 225

Alakazam ✎

HP 32/32

Psychic	38.65kg	1.35 m
Type	Weight	Height

5297
STARDUST

6
ABRA CANDY

POWER UP 600 1

BEST QUICK MOVE
Psycho Cut

BEST POWER MOVE
Psychic

STRONG AGAINST
● ●

WEAK AGAINST
● ●

066 MACHOP

CP 164

Machop ✎

HP 46/46

Fighting	18.75 kg	1.68 m
Type	Weight	Height

110
STARDUST

3
MACHOP CANDY

POWER UP 600 1

BEST QUICK MOVE
Low Kick

BEST POWER MOVE
Cross Chop

STRONG AGAINST
○ ● ● ●

WEAK AGAINST
● ● ●

067 MACHOKE

CP 270

Machoke ✎

HP 52/52

Fighting	77.04 kg	1.68 m
Type	Weight	Height

600
STARDUST

23
MACHOP CANDY

POWER UP 600 1

BEST QUICK MOVE
Low Kick

BEST POWER MOVE
Cross Chop

STRONG AGAINST
○ ● ● ●

WEAK AGAINST
● ● ●

068 MACHAMP

CP 687

Machamp ✎

HP 81/81

Fighting	166.34 kg	1.68 m
Type	Weight	Height

6882
STARDUST

40
MACHOP CANDY

POWER UP 1000 1

BEST QUICK MOVE
Karate Chop

BEST POWER MOVE
Cross Chop

STRONG AGAINST
○ ● ● ●

WEAK AGAINST
● ● ●

KEY	○ Normal	● Grass	● Dragon	● Rock
	● Water	● Flying	● Poison	● Fairy

069 BELLSPROUT

CP 357

Bellsprout ✎

HP 50 / 50

Grass / Poison	3.14 kg	0.6 m
Type	Weight	Height

⚑ 110   ● 21

BEST QUICK MOVE
Vine Whip

BEST POWER MOVE
Power Whip

STRONG AGAINST
● ●

WEAK AGAINST
● ● ● ●

CP 297

Weepinbell

HP 45 / 45

Grass / Poison	8.16 kg �XᴸL	1.17 m
Type	Weight	Height

⚑ 43813   ● 37
STARDUST   BELLSPROUT CANDY

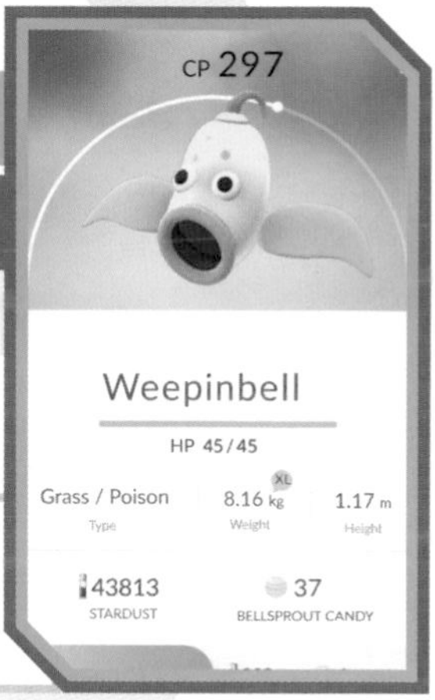

070 WEEPINBELL

BEST QUICK MOVE
Razor Leaf

BEST POWER MOVE
Power Whip

STRONG AGAINST
● ●

WEAK AGAINST
● ● ● ●

---

071 VICTREEBEL

CP 34

Victreebel ✎

HP 16 / 16

Grass / Poison	14.5 kg	1.63 m
Type	Weight	Height

⚑ 3603   ● 10
STARDUST   BELLSPROUT CANDY

BEST QUICK MOVE
Razor Leaf

BEST POWER MOVE
Solar Beam

STRONG AGAINST
● ●

WEAK AGAINST
● ● ● ●

CP 90

Tentacool ✎

HP 23 / 23

Water / Poison	34.21 kg	0.86 m
Type	Weight	Height

⚑ 110   ● 15
STARDUST   TENTACOOL CANDY

POWER UP   ⚑ 400   ● 1

072 TENTACOOL

BEST QUICK MOVE
Bubble

BEST POWER MOVE
Water Pulse

STRONG AGAINST
● ●

WEAK AGAINST
● ●

○ Electric	● Psychic	● Fighting	● Bug	● Ice
● Fire	● Ghost	● Ground	○ Steel	

073 TENTACRUEL

CP 686

BEST QUICK MOVE
Poison Jab

BEST POWER MOVE
Hydro Pump

STRONG AGAINST
● ●

WEAK AGAINST
● ● ○

Tentacruel ✎

HP 75/75

Water / Poison	48.88 kg	1.55 m
Type	Weight	Height

🌟 6782
STARDUST

🍬 3
TENTACOOL CANDY

POWER UP 🌟 1300 🍬 2

074 GEODUDE

CP 120

Geodude ✎

HP 28/28

Rock / Ground	28.38 kg	0.5 m
Type	Weight	Height

🌟 110
STARDUST

🍬 14
GEODUDE CANDY

POWER UP 🌟 600 🍬 1

BEST QUICK MOVE
Rock Throw

BEST POWER MOVE
Rock Slide

STRONG AGAINST
● ● ● ○

WEAK AGAINST
● ● ● ● ● ●

075 GRAVELER

BEST QUICK MOVE
Mud Slap

BEST POWER MOVE
Stone Edge

STRONG AGAINST
● ● ● ○ ●

WEAK AGAINST
● ● ● ● ● ●

CP 17

Graveler ✎

HP 10/10

Rock / Ground	60.3 kg	0.77 m
Type	Weight	Height

🌟 1414
STARDUST

🍬 10
GEODUDE CANDY

076 GOLEM

CP 482

Golem ✎

HP 60/60

Rock / Ground	275.6 kg	1.44 m
Type	Weight	Height

🌟 500
STARDUST

🍬 14
GEODUDE CANDY

🌟 800 🍬 1

BEST QUICK MOVE
Mud Slap

BEST POWER MOVE
Stone Edge

STRONG AGAINST
● ● ● ○

WEAK AGAINST
● ● ● ● ●

POKÉMON GO EXPERT BATTLE GUIDE

KEY	○ Normal	● Grass	● Dragon	● Rock
	● Water	● Flying	● Poison	● Fairy

077 PONYTA

BEST QUICK MOVE
Ember

BEST POWER MOVE
Fire Blast

STRONG AGAINST
● ● ● ●

WEAK AGAINST
● ● ●

Ponyta ✎
HP 38 / 38

Fire	42.55 kg	1.13 m
Type	Weight	Height

🏺 16828 STARDUST   🍬 12 PONYTA CANDY

POWER UP   🏺 800   🍬 1

078 RAPIDASH

BEST QUICK MOVE
Ember

BEST POWER MOVE
Fire Blast

STRONG AGAINST
● ● ● ●

WEAK AGAINST
● ● ●

Rapidash ✎
HP 46 / 46

Fire	135.92 kg	2.1 m
Type	Weight	Height

🏺 5239 STARDUST   🍬 18 PONYTA CANDY

POWER UP   🏺 600   🍬 1

079 SLOWPOKE

CP 239

BEST QUICK MOVE
Water Gun

BEST POWER MOVE
Psychic

STRONG AGAINST
● ● ● ● ●

WEAK AGAINST
● ● ●

Slowpoke ✎
HP 72 / 72

Water / Psychic	15.24 kg	1.01 m
Type	Weight	Height

🏺 110 STARDUST   🍬 7 SLOWPOKE CANDY

POWER UP   🏺 800   🍬 1

080 SLOWBRO

BEST QUICK MOVE
Water Gun

BEST POWER MOVE
Psychic

STRONG AGAINST
● ● ● ● ●

WEAK AGAINST
● ● ●

CP 256

Slowbro ✎
HP 49 / 49

Water / Psychic	110.49 kg	1.77 m
Type	Weight	Height

🏺 4288 STARDUST   🍬 3 SLOWPOKE CANDY

🏺 400

○ Electric	● Psychic	● Fighting	● Bug	● Ice
● Fire	● Ghost	● Ground	● Steel	

081 MAGNEMITE

CP 11

BEST QUICK MOVE
Spark

BEST POWER MOVE
Thunderbolt

STRONG AGAINST

WEAK AGAINST

Magnemite ✎

HP 10/10

Electric / Steel	6.54 kg	0.29 m
Type	Weight	Height

🔹3500
STARDUST

⬤ 3
MAGNEMITE CANDY

POWER UP 200 ⬤1

CP 99

Magneton ✎

HP 19/19

Electric / Steel	68.1 kg	1.04 m
Type	Weight	Height

🔹100
STARDUST

⬤ 5
MAGNEMITE CANDY

POWER UP 200 ⬤1

082 MAGNETON

BEST QUICK MOVE
Spark

BEST POWER MOVE
Flash Cannon

STRONG AGAINST

WEAK AGAINST

083 FARFETCH'D

CP 16

BEST QUICK MOVE
Cut

BEST POWER MOVE
Leaf Blade

STRONG AGAINST

WEAK AGAINST

Farfetch'd ✎

HP 10/10

Normal / Flying	17.57 kg	0.83 m
Type	Weight	Height

🔹6200
STARDUST

⬤ 6
FARFETCH'D CANDY

POWER UP 200 ⬤1

CP 31

Doduo ✎

HP 11/11

Normal / Flying	56.61 kg	1.57 m
Type	Weight	Height

🔹400
STARDUST

⬤ 3
DODUO CANDY

POWER UP 200 ⬤1

084 DODUO

BEST QUICK MOVE
Peck

BEST POWER MOVE
Drill Peck

STRONG AGAINST

WEAK AGAINST

KEY	◯ Normal	⬤ Grass	⬤ Dragon	⬤ Rock
	⬤ Water	⬤ Flying	⬤ Poison	⬤ Fairy

085 DODRIO

CP 356

Dodrio ✏

HP 46 / 46

Normal / Flying	72.42 kg	1.6 m
Type	Weight	Height

🔹110
STARDUST

● 107
DODUO CANDY

🔹800 ● 1

BEST QUICK MOVE
Feint Attack

BEST POWER MOVE
Drill Peck

STRONG AGAINST
● ● ●

WEAK AGAINST
● ● ●

086 SEEL

CP 13

Seel ✏

HP 13 / 13

Water	101.64 kg	1.13 m
Type	Weight	Height

🔹700
STARDUST

● 3
SEEL CANDY

POWER UP 🔹200 ● 1

BEST QUICK MOVE
Ice Shard

BEST POWER MOVE
Aqua Tail

STRONG AGAINST
● ● ●

WEAK AGAINST
●

087 DEWGONG

CP 145

Dewgong ✏

HP 40 / 40

Water / Ice	90.92 kg	1.47 m
Type	Weight	Height

🔹2600
STARDUST

● 3
SEEL CANDY

POWER UP 🔹400 ● 1

BEST QUICK MOVE
Frost Breath

BEST POWER MOVE
Blizzard

STRONG AGAINST
● ● ●

WEAK AGAINST
● ● ●

088 GRIMER

CP 80

Grimer ✏

HP 34 / 34

Poison	23.55 kg	0.76 m
Type	Weight	Height

🔹762
STARDUST

● 3
GRIMER CANDY

POWER UP 🔹400 ● 1

BEST QUICK MOVE
Poison Jab

BEST POWER MOVE
Sludge Bomb

STRONG AGAINST
● ●

WEAK AGAINST
● ●

○ Electric	● Psychic	● Fighting	● Bug	● Ice
● Fire	● Ghost	● Ground	○ Steel	

089 MUK

CP 226

Muk ✏

HP 51 / 51

Poison	30.49 kg	1.24 m
Type	Weight	Height

🦴 166
STARDUST

🍬 2
GRIMER CANDY

POWER UP   🦴 400   🍬 1

BEST QUICK MOVE
Poison Jab

BEST POWER MOVE
Gunk Shot

STRONG AGAINST
● ●

WEAK AGAINST
● ●

090 SHELLDER

CP 103

Shellder ✏

HP 20 / 20

Water	2.9 kg	0.27 m
Type	Weight	Height

🦴 12600
STARDUST

🍬 3
SHELLDER CANDY

🦴 600   🍬 1

BEST QUICK MOVE
Tackle

BEST POWER MOVE
Water Pulse

STRONG AGAINST
● ● ●

WEAK AGAINST
● ●

091 CLOYSTER

CP 356

Cloyster ✏

HP 38 / 38

Water / Ice	145.49 kg	1.61 m
Type	Weight	Height

🦴 231
STARDUST

🍬 2
SHELLDER CANDY

POWER UP   🦴 600   🍬 1

BEST QUICK MOVE
Frost Breath

BEST POWER MOVE
Blizzard

STRONG AGAINST
● ● ●

WEAK AGAINST
● ● ●

092 GASTLY

CP 390

Gastly ✏

HP 37 / 37

Ghost / Poison	0.11 kg	1.32 m
Type	Weight	Height

🦴 43813
STARDUST

🍬 6
GASTLY CANDY

BEST QUICK MOVE
Lick

BEST POWER MOVE
Sludge Bomb

STRONG AGAINST
● ● ●

WEAK AGAINST
● ● ●

KEY

○ Normal	● Grass	● Dragon	● Rock
● Water	● Flying	● Poison	● Fairy

093 HAUNTER

CP 161

Haunter ✎

HP 28/28

| Ghost / Poison | 0.08 kg | 1.57 m |
| Type | Weight | Height |

🔹 5240
STARDUST

🍬 4
GASTLY CANDY

BEST QUICK MOVE
Shadow Claw

BEST POWER MOVE
Sludge Bomb

STRONG AGAINST
● ● ●

WEAK AGAINST
● ● ●

094 GENGAR

CP 390

Gengar ✎

HP 45/45

| Ghost / Poison | 29.74 kg | 1.24 m |
| Type | Weight | Height |

🔹 586
STARDUST

🍬 18
GASTLY CANDY

BEST QUICK MOVE
Shadow Claw

BEST POWER MOVE
Sludge Bomb

STRONG AGAINST
● ● ●

WEAK AGAINST
● ● ●

095 ONIX

CP 79

Onix ✎

HP 19/19

| Rock / Ground | 221.53 kg | 9.6 m |
| Type | Weight | Height |

🔹 762
STARDUST

🍬 3
ONIX CANDY

BEST QUICK MOVE
Rock Throw

BEST POWER MOVE
Stone Edge

STRONG AGAINST
● ● ● ○ ●

WEAK AGAINST
● ● ● ● ● ●

096 DROWZEE

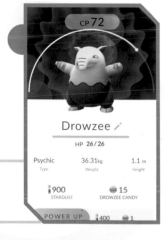

CP 72

Drowzee ✎

HP 26/26

| Psychic | 36.31 kg | 1.1 m |
| Type | Weight | Height |

🔹 900
STARDUST

🍬 15
DROWZEE CANDY

POWER UP   🔹 400   🍬 1

BEST QUICK MOVE
Pound

BEST POWER MOVE
Psychic

STRONG AGAINST
● ●

WEAK AGAINST
● ●

| ○ Electric | ● Psychic | ● Fighting | ● Bug | ● Ice |
| ● Fire | ● Ghost | ● Ground | ○ Steel | |

097 HYPNO

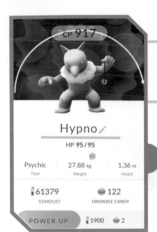

CP 917

BEST QUICK MOVE
Zen Headbutt

BEST POWER MOVE
Psychic

STRONG AGAINST
● ●

WEAK AGAINST
● ●

Hypno

HP 95/95

Psychic	27.88 kg	1.36 m
Type	Weight	Height

🔹61379
STARDUST

🍬122
DROWZEE CANDY

POWER UP 🔹1900 🍬2

098 KRABBY

CP 190

BEST QUICK MOVE
Bubble

BEST POWER MOVE
Water Pulse

STRONG AGAINST
● ● ●

WEAK AGAINST
● ●

Krabby

HP 29/29

Water	7.21 kg	0.41 m
Type	Weight	Height

🔹110
STARDUST

🍬25
KRABBY CANDY

POWER UP 🔹1000 🍬1

099 KINGLER

CP 371

BEST QUICK MOVE
Metal Claw

BEST POWER MOVE
X Scissor

STRONG AGAINST
● ● ●

WEAK AGAINST
● ●

Kingler

HP 41/41

Water	55.32 kg	1.31 m
Type	Weight	Height

🔹787
STARDUST

🍬9
KRABBY CANDY

POWER UP 🔹800 🍬1

100 VOLTORB

CP 84

BEST QUICK MOVE
Spark

BEST POWER MOVE
Thunderbolt

STRONG AGAINST
● ●

WEAK AGAINST
●

Voltorb

HP 23/23

Electric	10.19 kg	0.51 m
Type	Weight	Height

🔹110
STARDUST

🍬3
VOLTORB CANDY

🔹400 🍬1

KEY

○ Normal	● Grass	● Dragon	● Rock
● Water	● Flying	● Poison	● Fairy

101 ELECTRODE

BEST QUICK MOVE
Spark

BEST POWER MOVE
Hyperbeam

STRONG AGAINST

WEAK AGAINST

CP 549

Electrode 🖊

HP 62/62

Electric	13.04 kg	1.21 m
Type	Weight	Height

762
STARDUST

16
VOLTORB CANDY

POWER UP   1300   2

102 EXEGGCUTE

BEST QUICK MOVE
Confusion

BEST POWER MOVE
Psychic

STRONG AGAINST

WEAK AGAINST

CP 373

Exeggcute 🖊

HP 58/58

Grass / Psychic	2.46 kg	0.35 m
Type	Weight	Height

110
STARDUST

19
EXEGGCUTE CANDY

103 EXEGGUTOR

BEST QUICK MOVE
Zen Headbutt

BEST POWER MOVE
Solar Beam

STRONG AGAINST

WEAK AGAINST

CP 896

Exeggutor 🖊

HP 89/89

Grass / Psychic	36.81 kg	2.21 m
Type	Weight	Height

43813
STARDUST

12
EXEGGCUTE CANDY

104 CUBONE

BEST QUICK MOVE
Mud Slap

BEST POWER MOVE
Bone Club

STRONG AGAINST

WEAK AGAINST

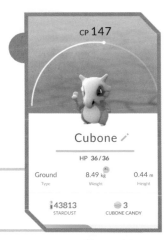

CP 147

Cubone 🖊

HP 36/36

Ground	8.49 kg	0.44 m
Type	Weight	Height

43813
STARDUST

3
CUBONE CANDY

○ Electric	● Psychic	● Fighting	● Bug	● Ice
● Fire	● Ghost	● Ground	○ Steel	

105 MAROWAK

CP 900

Marowak ✎

HP 77/77

Ground	11.62 kg	1.03 m
Type	Weight	Height

10592
STARDUST

5
CUBONE CANDY

BEST QUICK MOVE
Mud Slap

BEST POWER MOVE
Earthquake

STRONG AGAINST
● ● ● ○

WEAK AGAINST
● ● ●

106 HITMONLEE

CP 554

Hitmonlee ✎

HP 56/56

Fighting	57.54 kg	1.65 m
Type	Weight	Height

10347
STARDUST

18
HITMONLEE CANDY

POWER UP   1900   2

BEST QUICK MOVE
Rock Smash

BEST POWER MOVE
Stone Edge

STRONG AGAINST
○ ● ● ●

WEAK AGAINST
● ● ●

107 HITMONCHAN

CP 62

Hitmonchan ✎

HP 16/16

Fighting	38.61 kg	1.28 m
Type	Weight	Height

2700
STARDUST

3
HITMONCHAN CANDY

200   1

BEST QUICK MOVE
Rock Smash

BEST POWER MOVE
Brick Break

STRONG AGAINST
○ ● ● ●

WEAK AGAINST
● ● ●

108 LICKITUNG

CP 332

Lickitung ✎

HP 68/68

Normal	70.04 kg	1.33 m
Type	Weight	Height

110
STARDUST

15
LICKITUNG CANDY

POWER UP   800   1

BEST QUICK MOVE
Zen Headbutt

BEST POWER MOVE
Hyper Beam

STRONG AGAINST

WEAK AGAINST
●

KEY	○ Normal	● Grass	● Dragon	● Rock
	● Water	● Flying	● Poison	● Fairy

109 KOFFING

BEST QUICK MOVE
Tackle

BEST POWER MOVE
Sludge Bomb

STRONG AGAINST
● ●

WEAK AGAINST
● ●

CP 199

Koffing ✎

HP 27 / 27

Poison
Type

0.84 kg
Weight

0.59 m
Height

110
STARDUST

3
KOFFING CANDY

POWER UP   800   1

CP 242

Weezing ✎

HP 37 / 37

Poison
Type

8.33 kg
Weight

1.18 m
Height

269
STARDUST

2
KOFFING CANDY

POWER UP   400   1

110 WEEZING

BEST QUICK MOVE
Tackle

BEST POWER MOVE
Sludge Bomb

STRONG AGAINST
● ●

WEAK AGAINST
● ●

111 RHYHORN

CP 116

Rhyhorn ✎

HP 44 / 44

Ground / Rock
Type

90.93 kg
Weight

0.98 m
Height

110
STARDUST

3
RHYHORN CANDY

BEST QUICK MOVE
Mud Slap

BEST POWER MOVE
Stomp

STRONG AGAINST
● ● ● ● ● ●

WEAK AGAINST
● ● ● ●

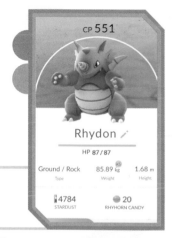

CP 551

Rhydon ✎

HP 87 / 87

Ground / Rock
Type

85.89 kg
Weight

1.68 m
Height

4784
STARDUST

20
RHYHORN CANDY

112 RHYDON

BEST QUICK MOVE
Mud Slap

BEST POWER MOVE
Stone Edge

STRONG AGAINST
● ● ● ● ● ●

WEAK AGAINST
● ● ● ●

Electric	Psychic	Fighting	Bug	Ice
Fire	Ghost	Ground	Steel	

113 CHANSEY

CP 28

Chansey ✎

HP 84/84

Normal	35.65 kg	1.09 m
Type	Weight	Height

471 STARDUST   ● 32 CHANSEY CANDY

POWER UP   ▮200   ● 1

BEST QUICK MOVE
Pound

BEST POWER MOVE
Hyper Beamin

STRONG AGAINST

WEAK AGAINST
●

114 TANGELA

BEST QUICK MOVE
Vine Whip

BEST POWER MOVE
Solar Beam

STRONG AGAINST
● ● ●

WEAK AGAINST
● ● ● ● ●

CP 431

Tangela ✎

HP 56/56

Grass	35.33 kg	0.99 m
Type	Weight	Height

110 STARDUST   ● 4 TANGELA CANDY

115 KANGASKHAN

CP 204

Kangaskhan ✎

HP 57/57

Normal	94.79 kg	2.29 m
Type	Weight	Height

884 STARDUST   ● 3 KANGASKHAN CANDY

POWER UP   ▮400   ● 1

BEST QUICK MOVE
Mud Slap

BEST POWER MOVE
Earthquake

STRONG AGAINST

WEAK AGAINST
●

116 HORSEA

BEST QUICK MOVE
Water Gun

BEST POWER MOVE
Dragon Pulse

STRONG AGAINST
● ● ●

WEAK AGAINST
●

CP 193

Horsea ✎

HP 29/29

Water	7.05 kg	0.39 m
Type	Weight	Height

110 STARDUST   ● 19 HORSEA CANDY

▮1000   ● 1

KEY   ○ Normal   ● Grass   ● Dragon   ● Rock
● Water   ● Flying   ● Poison   ● Fairy

117 SEADRA

BEST QUICK MOVE
Water Gun

BEST POWER MOVE
Hydro Pump

STRONG AGAINST

WEAK AGAINST

Seadra ✎

HP 60 / 60

Water	8.1 kg	1.18 m
Type	Weight	Height

43813
STARDUST

4
HORSEA CANDY

POWER UP   1900   2

118 GOLDEEN

BEST QUICK MOVE
Mud Shot

BEST POWER MOVE
Aqua Tail

STRONG AGAINST

WEAK AGAINST

Goldeen ✎

HP 46 / 46

Water	12.92 kg	0.63 m
Type	Weight	Height

43813
STARDUST

15
GOLDEEN CANDY

POWER UP   1600   2

119 SEAKING

BEST QUICK MOVE
Poison Jab

BEST POWER MOVE
Megahorn

STRONG AGAINST

WEAK AGAINST

Seaking ✎

HP 81 / 81

Water	31.2 kg	1.13 m
Type	Weight	Height

110
STARDUST

19
GOLDEEN CANDY

POWER UP   1600   2

120 STARYU

BEST QUICK MOVE
Water Gun

BEST POWER MOVE
Power Gem

STRONG AGAINST

WEAK AGAINST

Staryu ✎

HP 29 / 29

Water	38.44 kg	0.87 m
Type	Weight	Height

110
STARDUST

34
STARYU CANDY

POWER UP   1300   2

Electric	Psychic	Fighting	Bug	Ice
Fire	Ghost	Ground	Steel	

121 STARMIE

CP 775

Starmie ✎

HP 62 / 62

Water / Psychic	55.27 kg	1.36 m
Type	Weight	Height

🔹43813 STARDUST
🍬5 STARYU CANDY

BEST QUICK MOVE
Water Gun

BEST POWER MOVE
Hydro Pump

STRONG AGAINST
● ● ● ● ●

WEAK AGAINST
● ● ●

122 MR. MIME

CP 537

Mr. Mime ✎

HP 43 / 43

Psychic / Fairy	61.91 kg	1.29 m
Type	Weight	Height

🔹6817 STARDUST
🍬23 MR. MIME CANDY

POWER UP 🔹1600 🍬2

BEST QUICK MOVE
Zen Headbutt

BEST POWER MOVE
Psychic

STRONG AGAINST
● ●

WEAK AGAINST
● ● ●

123 SCYTHER

CP 767

Scyther ✎

HP 71 / 71

Bug / Flying	70.27 kg	1.66 m
Type	Weight	Height

🔹110
🍬7 SCYTHER CANDY

BEST QUICK MOVE
Steel Wing

BEST POWER MOVE
Bug Buzz

STRONG AGAINST
● ● ●

WEAK AGAINST
● ● ● ●

124 JYNX

CP 22

Jynx ✎

HP 12 / 12

Ice / Psychic	26.85 kg	1.22 m
Type	Weight	Height

🔹1000 STARDUST
●3 JYNX CANDY

🔹200 ●1

BEST QUICK MOVE
Frost Breath

BEST POWER MOVE
Psyshock

STRONG AGAINST
● ● ● ● ● ●

WEAK AGAINST
● ● ● ● ●

KEY
○ Normal
● Water
● Grass
● Flying
● Dragon
● Poison
● Rock
● Fairy

125 ELECTABUZZ

CP 118

Electabuzz ✎

HP 26 / 26

Electric	48.84 kg	1.35 m
Type	Weight	Height

⚡ 12281
STARDUST

🍬 0
ELECTABUZZ CANDY

🏅 200   🍬 1

BEST QUICK MOVE
Thundershock

BEST POWER MOVE
Thunder

STRONG AGAINST

WEAK AGAINST

126 MAGMAR

BEST QUICK MOVE
Ember

BEST POWER MOVE
Fire Blast

STRONG AGAINST

WEAK AGAINST

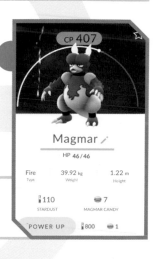

CP 407

Magmar ✎

HP 46 / 46

Fire	39.92 kg	1.22 m
Type	Weight	Height

⚡ 110
STARDUST

🍬 7
MAGMAR CANDY

POWER UP   🏅 800   🍬 1

127 PINSIR

CP 709

Pinsir ✎

HP 64 / 64

Bug	19.13 kg	1.17 m
Type	Weight	Height

⚡ 110
STARDUST

🍬 47
PINSIR CANDY

🏅 1300   🍬 2

BEST QUICK MOVE
Rock Smash

BEST POWER MOVE
X-Scissor

STRONG AGAINST

WEAK AGAINST

128 TAUROS

BEST QUICK MOVE
Tackle

BEST POWER MOVE
Earthquake

STRONG AGAINST

WEAK AGAINST

CP 187

Tauros ✎

HP 39 / 39

Normal	134.2 kg	1.71 m
Type	Weight	Height

⚡ 2000
STARDUST

🍬 3
TAUROS CANDY

🏅 400   🍬 1

⚪ Electric	🔵 Psychic	🟣 Fighting	🔵 Bug	⚪ Ice
🔴 Fire	🟣 Ghost	🟠 Ground	🔵 Steel	

129 MAGIKARP

BEST QUICK MOVE	**STRONG AGAINST**
Splash	● ● ●
BEST POWER MOVE	**WEAK AGAINST**
Struggle	● ●

Magikarp ✎
HP 25 / 25

Water	11.28 kg	0.95 m
Type	Weight	Height

110	40
STARDUST	MAGIKARP CANDY

POWER UP | 1600 | 2

130 GYARADOS

BEST QUICK MOVE	**STRONG AGAINST**
Bite	● ● ● ●
BEST POWER MOVE	**WEAK AGAINST**
Hydro Pump	● ●

Gyarados ✎
HP 119 / 119

Water / Flying	235kg	6.2 m
Type	Weight	Height

18977	16
STARDUST	MAGIKARP CANDY

POWER UP | 2500 | 2

131 LAPRAS

BEST QUICK MOVE	**STRONG AGAINST**
Frost Breath	● ● ●
BEST POWER MOVE	**WEAK AGAINST**
Blizzard	● ● ● ●

Lapras ✎
HP 111 / 111

Water / Ice	285.71 kg	2.91 m
Type	Weight	Height

1024	19
STARDUST	LAPRAS CANDY

POWER UP | 1000 | 1

NOT YET DISCOVERED

132 DITTO

BEST QUICK MOVE	**STRONG AGAINST**
Not yet known	Not yet known
BEST POWER MOVE	**WEAK AGAINST**
Not yet known	●

KEY	○ Normal	● Grass	● Dragon	● Rock
	● Water	● Flying	● Poison	● Fairy

133 EEVEE

CP 300

Eevee ✏

HP 52 / 52

Normal	7.6 kg	0.3 m
Type	Weight	Height

🔷110
STARDUST

🍬6
EEVEE CANDY

POWER UP   🔷1000   🍬1

BEST QUICK MOVE
Tackle

BEST POWER MOVE
Body Slam

STRONG AGAINST

WEAK AGAINST
⬤

134 VAPOREON

CP 692

Vaporeon ✏

HP 109 / 109

Water	4.87 kg	0.95 m
Type	Weight	Height

🔷2071
STARDUST

🍬1
EEVEE CANDY

POWER UP   🔷1000   🍬1

BEST QUICK MOVE
Water Gun

BEST POWER MOVE
Hydro Pump

STRONG AGAINST
⬤ ⬤ ⬤

WEAK AGAINST
⬤

135 JOLTEON

CP 1011

Jolteon ✏

HP 81 / 81

Electric	6.49 kg	0.89 m
Type	Weight	Height

🔷7482
STARDUST

🍬0
EEVEE CANDY

POWER UP   🔷2200   🍬2

BEST QUICK MOVE
Thunder Shock

BEST POWER MOVE
Thunder

STRONG AGAINST
⬤ ⬤

WEAK AGAINST
⬤

136 FLAREON

CP 116

Flareon ✏

HP 24 / 24

Fire	4.57 kg	0.65 m
Type	Weight	Height

🔷110
STARDUST

🍬6
EEVEE CANDY

BEST QUICK MOVE
Ember

BEST POWER MOVE
Fire Blast

STRONG AGAINST
⬤ ⬤ ⬤ ⬤

WEAK AGAINST
⬤ ⬤ ⬤

⬤ Electric	⬤ Psychic	⬤ Fighting	⬤ Bug	⬤ Ice	
⬤ Fire	⬤ Ghost	⬤ Ground	⬤ Steel		

137 PORYGON

CP 516

BEST QUICK MOVE
Tackle

BEST POWER MOVE
Signal Beam

STRONG AGAINST

WEAK AGAINST

Porygon ✎
HP 62 / 62

Normal	29.33 kg	0.79 m
Type	Weight	Height

🍬 28327 STARDUST   ⬤ 1 PORYGON CANDY

POWER UP   🍬 1300   ⬤ 2

---

138 OMANYTE

BEST QUICK MOVE
Water Gun

BEST POWER MOVE
Ancient Power

STRONG AGAINST

WEAK AGAINST

CP 316

Omanyte ✎
HP 33 / 33

Rock / Water	5.27 kg	0.38 m
Type	Weight	Height

🍬 23737 STARDUST   ⬤ 3 OMANYTE CANDY

🍬 1300   ⬤ 2

---

139 OMASTAR

CP 758

BEST QUICK MOVE
Water Gun

BEST POWER MOVE
Hydro Pump

STRONG AGAINST

WEAK AGAINST

Omastar ✎
HP 71 / 71

Rock / Water	39.82 kg	1.88 m
Type	Weight	Height

🍬 41591   ⬤ 22 OMANYTE CANDY

🍬 1300   ⬤ 2

---

140 KABUTO

BEST QUICK MOVE
Scratch

BEST POWER MOVE
Aqua Jet

STRONG AGAINST

WEAK AGAINST

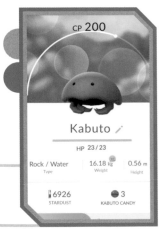

CP 200

Kabuto ✎
HP 23 / 23

Rock / Water	16.18 kg	0.56 m
Type	Weight	Height

🍬 6926 STARDUST   ⬤ 3 KABUTO CANDY

POKÉMON GO EXPERT BATTLE GUIDE

KEY   ◯ Normal   ⬤ Grass   ⬤ Dragon   ⬤ Rock
   ⬤ Water   ⬤ Flying   ⬤ Poison   ⬤ Fairy

141 KABUTOPS

BEST QUICK MOVE
Mud Shot

BEST POWER MOVE
Stone Edge

STRONG AGAINST

WEAK AGAINST

CP 788

Kabutops

HP 64 / 64

Rock / Water
Type

34.33 kg
Weight

1.15 m
Height

53762
STARDUST

3
KABUTO CANDY

142 AERODACTYL

BEST QUICK MOVE
Bite

BEST POWER MOVE
Hyper Beam

STRONG AGAINST

WEAK AGAINST

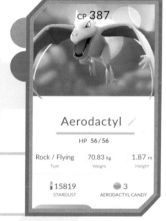

CP 387

Aerodactyl

HP 56 / 56

Rock / Flying
Type

70.83 kg
Weight

1.87 m
Height

15819
STARDUST

3
AERODACTYL CANDY

143 SNORLAX

BEST QUICK MOVE
Zen Headbutt

BEST POWER MOVE
Body Slam

STRONG AGAINST

WEAK AGAINST

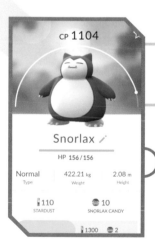

CP 1104

Snorlax

HP 156 / 156

Normal
Type

422.21 kg
Weight

2.08 m
Height

110
STARDUST

10
SNORLAX CANDY

1300   2

144 ARTICUNO

BEST QUICK MOVE
Not yet known

BEST POWER MOVE
Not yet known

STRONG AGAINST
Not yet known

WEAK AGAINST
Not yet known

**NOT YET
DISCOVERED**

Electric	Psychic	Fighting	Bug	Ice
Fire	Ghost	Ground	Steel	

145 ZAPDOS

BEST QUICK MOVE
Not yet known

BEST POWER MOVE
Not yet known

STRONG AGAINST
Not yet known

WEAK AGAINST
Not yet known

NOT YET DISCOVERED

NOT YET DISCOVERED

146 MOLTRES

BEST QUICK MOVE
Not yet known

BEST POWER MOVE
Not yet known

STRONG AGAINST
Not yet known

WEAK AGAINST
Not yet known

147 DRATINI

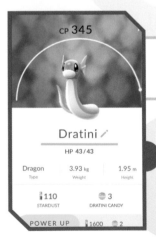

CP 345

Dratini ✏

HP 43/43

Dragon
Type

3.93 kg
Weight

1.95 m
Height

110
STARDUST

3
DRATINI CANDY

POWER UP   1600   2

BEST QUICK MOVE
Dragon Breath

BEST POWER MOVE
Aqua Tail

STRONG AGAINST
●

WEAK AGAINST
● ● ●

148 DRAGONAIR

BEST QUICK MOVE
Dragon Breath

BEST POWER MOVE
Dragon Pulse

STRONG AGAINST
●

WEAK AGAINST
● ● ●

CP 376

Dragonair ✏

HP 51/51

Dragon
Type

12.8 kg
Weight

3.76 m
Height

981
STARDUST

3
DRATINI CANDY

POWER UP   800   1

POKÉMON GO EXPERT BATTLE GUIDE

KEY   ○ Normal   ● Grass   ● Dragon   ● Rock
      ● Water   ● Flying ● Poison   ● Fairy

149 DRAGONITE

CP 1127

Dragonite ✐

HP 84 / 84

Dragon / Flying	383.32 kg	2.8 m
Type	Weight	Height

⬆8717
STARDUST

🍬 0
DRATINI CANDY

BEST QUICK MOVE
Dragon Breath

BEST POWER MOVE
Dragon Claw

STRONG AGAINST
● ● ●

WEAK AGAINST
● ● ● ●

NOT YET DISCOVERED

150 MEWTWO

BEST QUICK MOVE
Not yet known

BEST POWER MOVE
Not yet known

STRONG AGAINST
Not yet known

WEAK AGAINST
Not yet known

151 MEW

BEST QUICK MOVE
Not yet known

BEST POWER MOVE
Not yet known

STRONG AGAINST
Not yet known

WEAK AGAINST
Not yet known

NOT YET DISCOVERED

○ Electric	● Psychic	● Fighting	● Bug	○ Ice
● Fire	● Ghost	● Ground	● Steel	

When defending Gyms, a Pokémon
with a lower CP but a higher
defence and stamina stat may be a
better pick than a higher CP
Pokémon that just has a really high
attack. For attacking, don't worry
about picking a Pokémon with a
low defence score, you can
always just dodge.

MEASURING POKÉMON STRENGTH

STRENGTH BY NUMBERS

When battling in a Gym, you'll need to be able to learn to plan your battle strategy dodge incoming attacks, and choose your team wisely. Research from grassroots network The Silph Road ranks every pokémon by their best combined statistics, which should help you make the best decisions for your all-rounder team!

POKÉMON	BEST FAST MOVE	BEST SPECIAL MOVE	ATTACK	DEFENCE	STAMINA
Mewtwo	Psycho Cut	Psychic	284	202	212
Dragonite	Dragon Breath	Dragon Claw	250	212	182
Mew	Pound	Psychic	220	220	200
Arcticuno	Frost Breath	Blizzard	198	242	180
Snorlax	Lick	Hyper Beam	180	180	320
Moltres	Ember	Fire Blast	242	194	180
Zapdos	Thunder Shock	Thunder	232	194	180
Lapras	Frost Breath	Blizzard	186	190	260
Arcanine	Fire Fang	Fire Blast	230	180	180
Blastoise	Water Gun	Hydro Pump	186	222	158

POKÉMON	BEST FAST MOVE	BEST SPECIAL MOVE	ATTACK	DEFENCE	STAMINA
Vaporeon	Water Gun	Hydro Pump	186	168	260
Exeggcutor	Zen Headbutt	Solar Beam	232	164	190
Gyarados	Dragon Breath	Hydro Pump	192	196	190
Slowbro	Water Gun	Psychic	184	198	190
Venusaur	Vine Whip	Solar Beam	198	200	160
Poliwrath	Bubble	Hydro Pump	180	202	180
Flareon	Ember	Fire Blast	238	178	130
Muk	Poison Jab	Sludge Bomb	180	188	210
Charizard	Wing Attack	Fire Blast	212	182	156
Machamp	Karate Chop	Cross Chop	198	180	180
Vileplume	Razor Leaf	Solar Beam	202	190	150
Nidoqueen	Poison Jab	Earthquake	184	190	180
Golem	Mud Shot	Stone Edge	176	198	160
Omastar	Water Gun	Hydro Pump	180	202	140
Weezing	Tackle	Sludge Bomb	190	198	130
Nidoking	Poison Jab	Earthquake	204	170	162
Clefable	Pound	Moonblast	178	178	190
Victreebel	Razor Leaf	Solar Beam	222	152	160
Tentacruel	Poison Jab	Hydro Pump	170	196	160
Golduck	Water Gun	Hydro Pump	194	176	160
Hypno	Zen Headbutt	Psychic	162	196	170
Starmie	Water Gun	Hydro Pump	194	192	120
Ninetails	Ember	Fire Blast	176	194	146
Dewgong	Frost Breath	Blizzard	156	192	180
Cloyster	Frost Breath	Blizzard	196	196	100
Kabutops	Mud Shot	Stone Edge	190	190	120
Pinsir	Fury Cutter	X-Scissor	184	186	130
Rhydon	Mud Slap	Stone Edge	166	160	210
Magmar	Ember	Fire Blast	214	158	130
Rapidash	Ember	Fire Blast	200	170	130
Kangaskhan	Mud Slap	Earthquake	142	178	210
Jolteon	Thunder Shock	Thunder	192	174	130
Scyther	Steel Wing	Bug Buzz	176	180	140
Aerodactyl	Bite	Hyper Beam	182	162	160
Electabuzz	Thunder Shock	Thunder	198	160	130
Pidgeot	Wing Attack	Hurricane	170	166	166
Wigglytuff	Pound	Hyper Beam	168	108	280
Gengar	Shadow Claw	Sludge Wave	204	156	120
Magneton	Spark	Flash Cannon	186	180	100
Seaking	Poison Jab	Megahorn	172	160	160
Raichu	Spark	Thunder	200	154	120
Tauros	Tackle	Earthquake	148	184	150
Marowak	Mud Slap	Earthquake	140	202	120
Golbat	Wing Attack	Poison Fang	164	164	150
Kingler	Metal Claw	X-Scissor	178	168	110
Sandslash	Mud Shot	Earthquake	150	172	150
Hitmonchan	Rock Smash	Brick Break	138	204	100

Source: thesilphroad.com

POKÉMON	BEST FAST MOVE	BEST SPECIAL MOVE	ATTACK	DEFENCE	STAMINA
Venomoth	Bug Bite	Bug Buzz	172	154	140
Arbok	Bite	Gunk Shot	166	166	120
Parasect	Bug Bite	Solar Beam	162	170	120
Primeape	Low Kick	Cross Chop	178	150	130
Mr. Mime	Zen Headbutt	Psychic	154	196	80
Dodrio	Feint Attack	Drill Peck	182	150	120
Alakazam	Psycho Cut	Psychic	186	152	110
Electrode	Spark	Thunderbolt	150	174	120
Tangela	Vine Whip	Solar Beam	164	152	130
Wartortle	Water Gun	Hydro Pump	144	176	118
Dragonair	Dragon Breath	Dragon Pulse	170	152	122
Porygon	Tackle	Signal Beam	156	158	130
Likitung	Lick	Hyper Beam	126	160	180
Machoke	Low Kick	Cross Chop	154	144	160
Seadra	Water Gun	Hydro Pump	176	150	110
Gloom	Razor Leaf	Petal Blizzard	162	158	120
Fearow	Steel Wing	Drill Run	168	146	130
Ivysaur	Vine Whip	Solar Beam	156	158	120
Hitmonlee	Rock Smash	Stone Edge	148	172	100
Jynx	Pound	Psyshock	172	134	130
Persian	Scratch	Play Rough	156	146	130
Chansey	Pound	Psychic	40	60	500
Weepinbell	Razor Leaf	Sludge Bomb	190	110	130
Charmeleon	Scratch	Flamethrower	160	140	116
Graveler	Mud Shot	Stone Edge	142	156	110
Ponyta	Ember	Fire Blast	168	138	100
Raticate	Bite	Hyper Beam	146	150	110
Butterfree	Bug Bite	Bug Buzz	144	144	120
Nidorina	Poison Sting	Sludge Bomb	132	136	140
Beedrill	Bug Bite	Sludge Bomb	144	130	130
Omanyte	Water Gun	Brine	132	160	70
Poliwhirl	Bubble	Scald	132	132	130
Haunter	Lick	Sludge Bomb	172	118	90
Nidorino	Poison Sting	Sludge Bomb	142	128	122
Dugtrio	Mud Shot	Earthquake	148	140	70
Farfetch'd	Cut	Leaf Blade	138	132	104
Kabuto	Scratch	Aqua Jet	148	142	60
Koffing	Tackle	Sludge Bomb	136	142	80
Onix	Rock Throw	Stone Edge	90	186	70
Growlithe	Bite	Flamethrower	156	110	110
Grimer	Mud Slap	Sludge Bomb	124	110	160
Seel	Water Gun	Aqua Tail	104	138	130
Slowpoke	Water Gun	Psychic	110	110	180
Clefairy	Pound	Moonblast	116	124	140
Pidgeotto	Wing Attack	Aerial Ace	126	122	126
Rhyhorn	Mud Slap	Stomp	110	116	160
Oddish	Razor Leaf	Sludge Bomb	134	130	90

POKÉMON	BEST FAST MOVE	BEST SPECIAL MOVE	ATTACK	DEFENCE	STAMINA
Cubone	Mud Slap	Bone Club	102	150	100
Drowzee	Pound	Psychic	104	140	120
Exeggcute	Confusion	Psychic	110	132	120
Squirtle	Bubble	Aqua Tail	112	142	88
Kadabra	Psycho Cut	Shadow Ball	150	112	80
Eevee	Tackle	Body Slam	114	128	110
Bulbasaur	Vine Whip	Sludge Bomb	126	126	90
Psyduck	Water Gun	Cross Chop	132	112	100
Magnemite	Spark	Thunderbolt	128	138	50
Venonat	Bug Bite	Signal Beam	108	118	120
Staryu	Water Gun	Power Gem	130	128	60
Goldeen	Mud Shot	Aqua Tail	112	126	90
Tentacool	Bubble	Water Pulse	106	136	80
Machop	Low Kick	Cross Chop	118	96	140
Bellsprout	Vine Whip	Sludge Bomb	158	78	100
Paras	Bug Bite	Seed Bomb	122	120	70
Dratini	Dragon Breath	Aqua Tail	128	11	82
Charmander	Scratch	Flamethrower	128	108	78
Voltorb	Spark	Thunderbolt	102	124	80
Jigglypuff	Pound	Body Slam	98	54	230
Ditto	Pound	Struggle	110	110	96
Pikachu	Thunder Shock	Thunder	124	108	70
Geodude	Rock Throw	Rock Slide	106	118	80
Vulpix	Ember	Flamethrower	106	118	76
Shellder	Tackle	Water Pulse	120	112	60
Ekans	Poison Sting	Sludge Bomb	112	112	70
Nidoran - F	Poison Sting	Sludge Bomb	110	94	92
Mankey	Scratch	Cross Chop	122	96	80
Sandshrew	Mud Shot	Rock Slide	90	114	100
Doduo	Peck	Drill Peck	126	96	70
Krabby	Bubble	Water Pulse	116	110	60
Horsea	Water Gun	Dragon Pulse	122	100	60
Nidoran - M	Poison Sting	Sludge Bomb	100	104	110
Poliwag	Bubble	Body Slam	108	98	80
Gastly	Lick	Sludge Bomb	136	82	60
Meowth	Scratch	Body Slam	104	94	80
Pidgey	Tackle	Aerial Ace	94	90	80
Spearow	Peck	Drill Peck	102	78	80
Abra	Zen Headbutt	Psyshock	110	76	50
Zubat	Bite	Sludge Bomb	88	90	80
Rattata	Tackle	Body Slam	92	86	60
Diglett	Mud Shot	Dig	108	86	20
Metapod	Bug Bite	Struggle	56	86	100
Kakuna	Poison Jab	Struggle	62	82	90
Caterpie	Bug Bite	Struggle	62	66	90
Weedle	Bug Bite	Struggle	68	64	80
Magicarp	Splash	Struggle	42	84	40

Source: thesilphroad.com

POKÉMON GLOSSARY

AUGMENTED REALITY (AR) (1)

A live view of your physical environment, for example a street you're standing on, with superimposed computer-generated images, audio, and graphics.

ATTACK (ATK)

The moves that your chosen Pokémon make in a Gym battle against other Trainer's Pokémon.

BATTLE

When you go to a rival Gym or defend your own, you release the Pokémon of your choice and have it fight with other Pokémon.

CANDY

You can get Candies by catching Pokémon, hatching Eggs, or by transferring Pokémon to Professor Willow. Giving Candies to your Pokémon can strengthen or evolve them.

CHARGE ATTACK (POWER MOVE)

Once the charge bar is at full during a Pokémon battle, you can press down on the enemy for a few seconds and your Pokémon will deliver it's charged Power attack.

CP (COMBAT POWER)

Pokémon have a certain amount of CP when they are first captured. Generally the higher the CP stat, the better they are in battle. The max number of CP a Pokémon can have is dependent on Trainer level and the specific species of Pokémon.

DEFENDER BONUS

For joining a Gym and leaving one of

your Pokémon to defend it, a player will get Stardust and PokéCoins as a daily reward. Players can reap this reward at the PokéShop.

DODGING

The defensive move that you can direct your Pokémon to make during a battle to dodge your opponent's attakcs.

EGGS

Pokémon Eggs are found at PokéStops and can be granted when you level up. They can be hatched into Pokémon, if you do some walking first.

EVOLUTION

By giving your Pokémon enough Candies, they can evolve into stronger, rarer, and more powerful Pokémon.

GYMS (2)

Allied Gyms are controlled by members of your team. Rival Gyms

are controlled by members of other teams. In allied Gyms, you can train your Pokémon for XP and help teammates defend their spots. In rival Gyms, you battle your Pokémon for XP and control of the Gym.

HP (HIT POINTS)

Hit Points measure your Pokémon's health. If your Pokémon runs out of HP, it faints and can't fight until it's revived.

INCENSE (3)

You can use Incense, which you can buy at the shop or find at PokéStops, to attract Pokémon to your avatar.

INCUBATOR

If you want to hatch an Egg that you've collected, place it in the Incubator. After you walk a certain distance with the app open, the incubated Egg will hatch, adding a new Pokémon to your collection.

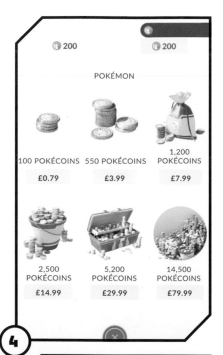

INDIVIDUAL VALUES (IV)

In Pokémon Go, there are three hidden stats or "individual values" that affect how strong Pokémon are in Gym battles. They are Attack, Defence, and Stamina. These "IV scores" affect both the species as a whole and individual Pokémon.

LEVELS

Every Trainer starts off at Level 1, but as they gather XP by catching Pokémon, evolving them, visiting PokéStops, and battling at Gyms, they can advance to higher levels. When a Trainer reaches a new level, they automatically receive rewards and also attract stronger, rarer Pokémon. This can help their Pokémon achieve higher CP scores.

LUCKY EGG

By using a Lucky Egg, you can double the number of XP you earn for 30 minutes, meaning you're the one who is actually lucky when you snag this item!

LURE MODULE

You can set up a Lure Module, which you can purchase at the shop or earn through levelling up. Activate one at a PokéStop, and it will bring Pokémon near that stop for 30 minutes. Anyone can see and use your Lure to their own advantage.

MEDALS (7)

You're awarded Medals throughout the game for various achievements, including collecting a set number of specific Pokémon types, or for walking certain distances.

POKÉMON

These are the creatures who are dominating your every waking moment. The name Pokémon is a play on the phrase "pocket monster", which is what they are!

POKÉBALL (6)

An item used to catch and contain Pokémon. You can find more PokéBalls at PokéStops or purchase them with PokéCoins. You can also get the Great Ball and Ultra Ball after reaching certain levels, which are each a step up from PokéBalls and can capture stronger Pokémon.

POKÉCOINS (4)

Pokémon Go's currency, with which you can purchase premium items. To get PokéCoins, buy them in the shop with real money or earn them by controlling Gyms.

POKÉDEX

An official directory of all the Pokémon and their stats.

POKÉSTOP (5)

A PokéStop is where you can collect free goods, such as Eggs, Potions, Incubators, and PokéBalls. PokéStops are usually placed in prominent public places, like train stations, churches, and landmarks.

POTIONS

You feed Potions to your Pokémon to heal them and restore their HP.

POWER-UP

In order to make your Pokémon more effective fighters in battle, Trainers can use Stardust and Candy to up their Pokémon's HP and CP.

PRESTIGE

As more allies train and win at a Gym, the Gym earns more Prestige, allowing it to level up and add more defenders, making it harder to capture.

QUICK MOVE

The regular attack your Pokémon will do in a Battle.

RAZZ BERRY (8)

By feeding this to a Pokémon during an encounter, it will be easier to catch and less likely to run away.

REVIVE

If your Pokémon faints during a battle, it needs to be brought back to life with a Revive, which you can start collecting after you reach Level 5.

STARDUST

Stardust is used to power up Pokémon. You can earn Stardust by catching Pokémon, hatching Eggs, or by protecting or training at a Gym.

TRAINERS

The people who play Pokémon Go.

TRAINING

You can train your Pokémon one at a time for XP in allied Gyms against the Pokémon of other players who also belong to your team.

TYPES

All Pokémon have one or two fighting types, such as Psychic or Water, that have strengths and weaknesses against other Pokémon types. Using knowledge about types, Trainers are able to strategize against opponents in battles.

XP (EXPERIENCE POINTS)

Experience Points measure your progress as a Trainer. If you hit a certain amount of XP, you will level up.

POKÉMON GO EXPERT BATTLE GUIDE

INDEX OF POKÉMON

INDEX

PICTURE CREDITS

While every effort has been made to credit all contributors, Weldon Owen would like to apologize should there have been any omissions or errors, and would be pleased to make any appropriate corrections for future editions of this book.

Shutterstock:
Shutterstock/Stoyan Yotov: p108; Shutterstock/Rokas Tenys: p 7; BlurryMe / Shutterstock.com: p153; Tawin Mukdharakosa/Shutterstock.com: p159;

All screenshots © Niantic, Inc.

Weldon Owen would like to thank:
Matt Yeo and Cloud King Productions, Lucy Kingett